1

The Anunnaki Series

Published by Times Square Press. Elite Associates
www.timessquarepress.com

*** *** ***

2022 Anunnaki Code: End Of The World And Their Return To Earth

Ulema Book of Parallel Dimension, Extraterrestrials and Akashic Records

4th Edition Edition

Maximillien de Lafayette

Editor

Virginia Velez

Acknowledgment and Gratitude

We are deeply grateful to the Honorable Anunnaki-Ulema who have generously contributed to this book:
Contributors:
Master Li
Ulema Sharif Al Mutawalli
Ulema Mordachai Ben Zvi
Ulema Sadik Bin Jaafar Al Kamali
Ulema F. Oppenheimer
Ulema A. Berkof
Ulema Ramash Govinda
Ulema Tabeth Al-Baydani
Ulema Shaul Sorenztein
Sinhar Ambar Anati
Ulema F. Tayara
Ulema Mirach Faridi Beraz
For without their guidance and contributions, this book would have remained stacks of papers in our drawer.

⌘ ⌘ ⌘

2022 Anunnaki Code: End Of The World And Their Return To Earth According to Maximillien de Lafayette

Ulema Book of Parallel Dimension, Extraterrestrials and Akashic Records

4th Edition

Maximillien de Lafayette

Editor

Virginia Velez

Elite Associates International. Times Square Press

2010

*** *** ***

Table of Contents

***   ***   ***

Prologue

This remarkable book has many facets, and is so extremely rich in content that trying to introduce it is not an easy task. The material is unique, to start with. Most of it has been learned from sources that are totally out of reach for the average reader – and even for many scholars.

Some of this material was hidden in the archives of museums, some written on tablets that have never been translated before, and some of it is oral knowledge that have never been given to a Westerner before. The author, Maximillien de Lafayette, have been so fortunate as to study with those who are the guardians of this knowledge in Lebanon, Egypt, Iraq, the islands of Arwad and Cyprus, and his travels even took him to the Far East, where he studied with Tibetan and Japanese teachers. This is the first time he is making use of this depot of knowledge, and we are very lucky to have access to it.

The subjects introduced in this book are explosive. Most important is the fact that it reveals the potential return of the Anunnaki in 2022, and the most frightening transformation that it would bring to the earth. If this is going to happen, a huge number of the people on earth, those grossly contaminated by Grays' DNA, will be annihilated. You know who they are – the child murderers, the rapists, those who torture, those who abuse, etc. Yes, we all know who they are. But the Anunnaki, who have no false sentimentality at all, will not tolerate even a medium level contamination.

Unless they do their best to clean themselves

during the grace period of the next fourteen years, those of mid level contamination will also be destroyed. Those who would manage to clean themselves to a certain degree may possibly (but without any guarantee) be able to escape the burning, smoking earth through special portals, called Ba'abs.

Only those who are naturally uncontaminated and those who managed to clean themselves completely will be taken up through an antimatter bubble, with the animals and certain important buildings and inanimate art and culture objects, and kept safe until the earth would be clean again. Such a scenario is, to say the least, disconcerting. Even if you are not sure whether you are a believer or not, you should certainly consider the possibilities – and the book teaches you exactly how to save yourself.

For those of us interested in the use of esoteric codes, they are here for you to learn. Each term will teach you how to use it for your benefit, how to apply it not only to your spiritual growth, but to your business, relationships, and daily life.

You will learn how to interpret the codes in many ancient languages, how to build a physical amulet/code that will protect certain aspects of your life, and how to develop your psychic and extrasensory powers by simply using these codes.

You will learn how the Anunnaki were our original creators, who else tempered with our genetic materials, and how God factors into all this. Religion, true and false, will be explored. Jesus, who never really died on the Cross, will be shown as a historical figure, with his wife, Mary Magdalene, with whom he escaped to ancient Marseille. Who were Adam and Eve? Who was the Serpent? How do the gods of Sumer signify to us?

You will be asked to consider the old theory, now discarded, that the Anunnaki came here to mine gold. You will meet the earliest civilization, and no, it was not Sumer. It was, believe it or not, Phoenicia! You will learn many secrets about the Anunnaki themselves – such as their extrasensory powers, their deep knowledge of genetics and science, and their unbelievably long lifespan.

Who is their God?

What kind of social classes they have?

What spiritual principles do they exercise?

And most important, what is their plan for humanity after the apocalyptic cleansing of the earth. Will they control our minds?

Will they change our lifestyle, our monetary system, and our businesses?

Space is allowed for respectfully examining the work of pioneer Anunnaki scholars and their past achievements. Much of it is still quite valid, other material must be discarded in view of new research. Science and technology is here to examine the question of the Anunnaki in their light.

And of course, the question always remains – how much science and technology has been given to earth governments already?

And if they were, how much of it is given by the vicious Grays, who have contaminated us from the early days until the present, drawing our blood for their experiments, in exchange for such science and technology, all the while dealing with unscrupulous governments all over the planet, including our own?

In the end of the book, you will find the Enuma Elish, the great poem that reveals so much about our past and which has been studied by all researches in quest of answers to the question of who really created the early human race.

As I was studying the book, I asked Mr. de Lafayette if there was more to it than what he has written in this book. "Of course," he said. "This is just the tip of the iceberg. I plan to continue working with this material, with more books to follow. I think the world now needs the wisdom expressed in this material." I could not agree with him more.

And yet, despite the uniqueness of this material, the book is entirely accessible. It is important to note that both the Ulema and the Anunnaki always feel that knowledge should be imparted in the most straightforward way, with a simple and down to earth approach. The teacher is never to complicate any data with esoteric, foolish jargon. The result is a book you can both enjoy and learn from – on many subtle levels.

The book is arranged in the time-honoured tradition of questions and answers. To me, it suggests a formula that has been enthusiastically embraced by students for many, many years. You can get the most from this book by studying one question and one answer each day.

Of course, some of the answers are short, some are long. But don't let the short ones deceive you into thinking that you can read two or three. Each question requires its own time, its own thinking. In this way, each question is much like a Japanese koan.

The simplicity of the question does not reveal the complexity of the answer. The long answers, on the other hand, could certainly be divided into a few days of reading.

By the time you have finished the book, you will be one of those lucky individuals who really understand the Ulema teaching, and the Anunnaki Code and its implications.

The return of the Anunnaki is not a new idea. It has been already announced in sacred scriptures, but of course interpreted differently. Some said Jesus is an Anunnaki, and he will return as a cosmic Messiah. A new school of religious thought in Iran suggests that Mohammed will return as a celestial being.

And we should not to forget the Rapture and the Gnostics as well. But all of them have their origin in the Anunnaki texts, because these texts were written thousands of years before the Old Testament, the New Testament, and the Quran. The book will explore this topic.

The author has told me that he hopes that the religious material, some of which is avant-guard to the extreme, will not offend anyone.

He is aware that much of it is different from all organized religions, but he hopes that the reader will approach this part of the book with an open mind, taking it away from Biblical context. Whether the depiction of God according to the author, contributors, the Ulema, the Sumerians, the Phoenicians, and the Anunnaki, differs from the Judeo-Christian concept, in essence, they all agree that there is a major force, a creative energy that had created the known and unknown cosmos.

In fact, it is only a semantic issue. The definition and understanding of God received many face lifts as theology adopted ancient and new beliefs and customs, and as science explored wider dimensions of knowledge and discoveries.

The Editorial Board

1-Is It True The Anunnaki Created Man From A Germ?

THE ANSWER

- The Sumerian texts tell us that the Anunnaki tried hard to create a perfect "working human".
- The very first 7 prototypes of man the Anunnaki created were not perfect. Humans lacked intelligence. They were unable to understand the instructions of the Anunnaki.
- The original intention of the Anunnaki was to create a specie of humans capable of carrying physical tasks without questioning their origin, the nature of their creators, and the reason for being created.
- The Anunnaki wanted to produce specie that can follow orders during the early phases of their enterprise on earth.
- The Anunnaki never intended to create a very "smart" human. They just needed "primitive workers" who could understand one thing: Do the job and follow the orders as the Anunnaki ask!

The Anunnaki combined their genes with the DNA of an existing human race, and vice-versa. However, several passages from the Sumerian texts tell a different story; early humans were created from the DNA of an Anunnaki who had the rank of a king, a ruler or a "god", that was blended with clay found in abundance in Sumer (Modern day, Iraq).

Later on in history, "clay" became" Tourab", dirt in Arabic, and "clay" also became "germ". The Quran referred to it.

Here is an excerpt from the Quran: "Is man not aware that We created him from a little germ?"

It is obvious that the Islamic text was written in accordance with the Sumerian-Anunnaki scriptures containing the following: "We first created man from an essence of clay; then placed him a living germ in a secure enclosure.

The germ we made a clot of blood, and the clot a lump of flesh. This we fashioned into bones, then clothed the bones with flesh..."

*** *** ***

2-Did The Anunnaki Come To Earth To Mine Gold?

The Answer

No, they did not! The Anunnaki are not cowboys in the West!
The Anunnaki are a very advanced race. They can transmute metals into gold anytime they want. To their scientists, it is a piece of cake.

- Besides, Ne.Be.ru, the real name of their planet is abundant with gold.
- A race that overcame the laws of physics of so many galaxies, conquered space-time travel, participated in the creation of the cosmos, and created the brain and body of so many races and humans should be considered advanced enough to conclude a very simple scientific transaction such as changing iron or copper into gold.
- Also, it is very important to remember that gold, even in a huge quantity cannot save a planet from deterioration and adjusting its weather and climate...
- They came to Earth for other reasons.

Why did the Anunnaki originally come to earth?

The Anunnaki did more than just come to earth. They have created it, million of years ago.
At that time, a group of Anunnaki scientists on Nibiru, including Inanna, Sinhar Anki (EN.KI), Anu, Enlil (Ilil)

etc. decided to extend their experiments in creating biological, living forms.

To do that, they needed a good plan and permission from the Council, so they worked it out and requested a meeting.

The Council considered their suggestions, and agreed that such work would greatly increase Anunnaki knowledge and therefore would be an excellent idea to pursue. However, they had one condition. The scientists were welcome to start working – but their laboratory would have to be off-planet.

The Council suspected that the introduction of new life forms, even in the isolated conditions of a laboratory, might be a threat to everyone already on Nibiru. Large and small animals, and particularly people that were to be created in the image of the Anunnaki, could not be tolerated to wander freely on Nibiru.

The scientists devoted more thought to their project, and agreed that what they really needed was a planet-sized laboratory, where the creations could interact in a controlled environment without the interference of previously existing life forms.

The solution, to which the Council readily agreed, was to create a planet specifically for the purpose. The Council added that they understood that it would be convenient to create the planet within the Milky Way, for easy traveling, but it had to be at some distance from Nibiru, just in case.

And so the scientists went to the edge of the galaxy, and caused a star to explode and create a solar system. The sun, which they named Shemesh (Sol) was surrounded by a few planets, and after a suitable amount of time (eons to us, but nothing to the Anunnaki who can play with time as they wish) went there to decide which planet would be the most appropriate.

For a short time they considered the planet we call Mars, which at the time had plenty of water (the most important ingredient necessary for the laboratory, after oxygen) but finally settled on choosing earth.

They went to earth, started creating the life forms, fostered the evolutionary process, and managed to accumulate an enormous amount of useful knowledge, all of which they telepathically transferred to Nibiru, where it was much appreciated.

Unfortunately, the knowledge leaked to the Grays at Zeta Reticuli, and they decided to use the humans, and sometimes the cattle, in their doomed experiments that were geared to save their own miserable race.

While doing this, they sadly contaminated the pure genetic material the Anunnaki so painstakingly created, and the humans that resulted were no longer suitable for the study.

That was the reason why the Anunnaki deserted their research on earth.

However, it is well known that the Anunnaki, which are a most responsible and compassionate race, did not lose interest in their creations, and have never quite deserted us to the Grays.

Most important, as a result of some additional knowledge revealed to them over the last forty years, they are planning a comeback to earth.

It is not clear if they are intending to continue their research, or if their coming is merely a benevolent attempt to clean the earth from all Grays' genetic material and reclaim us as better human beings, but either way, we will be made much happier, kinder, and more comfortable by the Anunnaki return.

The expectation is that they would formally announce it around 2022.

*** *** ***

3-What Is Ay'inbet?

The Answer

- **1-Origin:** Derived from the Phoenician Ay'inbet. 1-Ayin means eye, and Bet means house. In Hebrew, ayin is ayn and bet is beth. In Arabic, ayin is 'ayn, and bet is bayt (Written Arabic), and bet (Spoken Arabic). In Anakh (Anunnaki language), it is exactly the same; ayin is Ain, and bet is bet.

- **2-Numerical value:** 3.

- **3-Meaning:**
1-The eye of the house;
2-Main entrance of a home;
3-Protection of one's home. The upper class of the Anunnaki is ruled by Baalshalimroot.

His subjects are called "Shtaroout-Hxall Ain", meaning the inhabitants of the house of knowledge, or "those who see clearly." Their eyes are not similar to humans' eyes, because the Anunnaki do not have a retina.
Their physical eyes are used to perceive dimensional objects. While their "inner eye" sees multi-dimensional spheres. The process is created by the mind. The word "Ain" was later adopted by the early inhabitants of the Arab Peninsula.
"Ain" in Arabic means "eye".

The Badou Rouhal (Nomads) of the Arabs who lived in the Sahara considered the "eye" to be the most important feature of the face.

Those who have practiced "Al Sihr" (Magic) used their eyes as a psychic conduit. In their magic rituals and séances, they close their eyes and let imageries inhabit their mind.

Once, the spirit called "Rouh, Jinn, Afrit" enters the body, the eyes open up and the vision is henceforth activated by the spirit.And what they saw next was called "Rou'Yah", meaning "visions".

In the secret teachings of Sufism, visions of Al Hallaj, and of the greatest poetess of Sufism, Rabiha' Al Adawi Yah, known also as "Ha Chi katou Al Houbb Al Ilahi" (The mistress of the divine love), and in the banned book *Shams Al Maa'Ref Al Kubrah* (Book of the Sun of the Great Knowledge), the word "eye" meant the ultimate knowledge, or wisdom from above.

"Above" clearly indicates the heavens. In the pre-Islamic era, heavens meant the spheres where the creators of the universe live. This sphere was shared by good gods and evil gods. The concept of hell was unknown to the pagan Badou Rouhal.

Later on in history, when Islam invaded the Arab world, the "eye" became the symbol of Allah, the god of the Muslims.

In modern times, several secret esoteric societies and cultures adopted the "eye" as an institutional symbol and caused it to appear on many edifices' pillars, bank notes, money bills (including the US Dollar), and religious texts.

In ancient times, the Anunnaki eye was a very powerful symbol of the favorite regional god. It appeared on Egyptian, Sumerian, Persian, and Phoenician pillars and tablets.

The Phoenicians of the city of Amrit and the Island of Arwad, considered to be direct descendants of the Anunnaki, engraved the Anunnaki eye on altars dedicated to gods' healing powers.

- **4-Code/Use according to mythology and esoterism:** To be written three times on a piece of leather or cloth and hidden in the left pocket.

- **5-Benefits:**
1-Safe return to home-base;
   2-Against forced eviction.
   3-Protection of one's property. 4-Peace at home.

- **6-Geometrical presentation/Symbol:** Circle. In spiritual-mental séances, the circle becomes a triangle.

*** *** ***

4-What Is Za.Yin?

The Answer

- **1-Origin:** Derived from the Phoenician Zayin.
Same pronunciation in Aramaic, Syriac, Hebrew, and Arabic. In Anakh (Anunnaki language), it is Za. YIL.

- **2-Numerical value:** 7.

- **3-Meaning:** Weapon.

- **4-Code/Use according to mythology and esoterism:** To be written seven times on a small stone and placed inside the house, more precisely in the foyer of the house.
On the road, it is advised to grab it in your right palm, and repeat the name of the opposition seven times. Once done, you keep it in your right pocket. During mental communication, you draw a circle and you place the stone on the left side of the circle, facing north.

- **5-Benefits:** 1-Defense against intruders; 2-To overcome or change a negative decision by a third party that can affect your well-being and/or assets; 3-Helpful in negotiations and while giving a speech, lecture or a presentation.

- **6-Geometrical presentation/Symbol:**
Two adjacent triangles.

5-What Is Resh-Aal?

The Answer

- **1-Origin:** Derived from the Phoenician Resh. Same pronunciation in Aramaic, Sumerian, Babylonian, and Syriac. In Arabic, it is pronounced "Ras." In Hebrew, it is pronounced "Rosh". In Anakh (Anunnaki language), it is "Rash.El." All have the same meaning.

- **2-Numerical value:** 20.

- **3-Meaning:** Head.

- **4-Code/Use according to mythology and esoterism:** To be written with "Zaa' Fa. Ran" liquid, once in the center of your left palm.

- **5-Benefits:** 1-Will heal headaches in less than 10 minutes; 2-In official meetings, and before anybody else enters the room, write it twice on your seat.

- **6-Geometrical presentation/Symbol:** A circle inside a square.

*** *** ***

6-What Is Sam.Ekh?

The Answer

Sam Ekh

- **1-Origin**: Derived from the Phoenician Samekh. Same pronunciation in Aramaic, Syriac, and Hebrew. No equivalent in Arabic. In Anakh (Anunnaki language), it is SA.Ek'h.

- **2-Numerical value:** 15.

- **3-Meaning:** Pillar.

- **4-Code/Use according to mythology and esoterism:** To be drawn in the form of three parallel lines in any direction.

- **5-Benefits:** 1-Much needed to open an oracle.

- **6-Geometrical presentation/Symbol:**
  Three parallel lines of the same length.

***   ***   ***

7-What Is Or Who Is ABD?

The Answer

Abd

- **1-Origin:** Derived from the Arabic Abd. In Anakh (Anunnaki language), it is SA.Ek'h.

- **2-Numerical value:** 13.

- **3-Meaning:** It was the first name given to the first genetically created human by the Anunnaki. It means the same thing in Sumerian, Babylonian, ancient and modern Arabic and Anakh (Anunnaki language). The original meaning is "Slave", later on; Enki changed it to "Servant". In contemporary Arabic, the word "Abed" means two things: 1-A black person; 2: A slave. You will find many clues in the Arabic poems of Abu Al Tib Al Mutanabbi, and in the writings of Abu Al Ala' Al Maari (died in 1057), and Al-Nabigha Al-Zoubyani (535-604), and in the story of king Dabshalim and Brahman Baydaba. (Around 175 B.C.)

- **4-Code/Use according to mythology and esoterism:** Never to be used, written, or pronounced.

- **5-Benefits:** Negative effects. Bad expectations.

- **6-Geometrical presentation/Symbol:** Reverse cross inside a triangle.

8-What Is Adala?
Is It Karma?

The Answer

Adala

- **1-Origin:** Derived from the Anunnaki language, Ada. LA.

- **2-Numerical value:** 100.

- **3-Meaning:** As defined in the "Anunnaki Encyclopedia"; In Anakh (Anunnaki language) term for karma.

Although the Anunnaki do not believe in religions as we do on earth, their sense and understanding of ethics, justice, good and evil deeds, and merits are well developed.

The Anunnaki have families, parents, children, social ethics and laws. They see the universe, the development of mind and character's evolvement quite differently from the way we do. They take into a great consideration the consequences of an act, even a thought.

The Anunnaki do not have courts of law, trials, tribunals, prosecutors, judges, lawyers and corporal punishment, but they have established rules that govern behavior, merits, deeds, and social justice.

However, karma is not a reward for deeds after death.

The Anunnaki do not believe in reincarnation, a spiritual life after death, the return of one's body, character and soul to Nibiru after death. It is difficult to explain the Anunnaki's karma in terrestrial terms.

But, basically, Anunnaki's karma is the place and function a deceased Anunnaki occupies and plays in a sphere existing beyond the one he/she left.

In contrast with karma on earth, all Anunnaki have the ability to change their karma and their next destination before they die. Even though, death does not exist in the Anunnaki's world, as we understand death on earth, all Anunnaki reach a point when and where the last cell of energy in their body ceases to function, thus resulting in the deterioration of their bodies.

After that, the Anunnaki body fades away, and the mind of the new Anunnaki occupies one of the doubles or copies of their minds and bodies.

It is at this critical moment when the karma becomes relevant. "Adala" has 2 levels:

A-Level one is a sphere of existence, where the Anunnaki ceases to evolve, and the "Conduit" is no longer fully operational.

The departed Anunnaki (some live 400,000 years) could still contact the community he/she once lived in, and communicate with parents and relatives, but the range of communication is minimal.

This happens when his/her deeds were not viewed by the Anunnaki Council as of the first order.

B-Level two is a sphere of ultimate development where the Anunnaki acquires a more developed and powerful personality.

This personality will have access to a new physical body and a greater "Conduit".

This happens when the Anunnaki Council has honored the good deeds of the departed Anunnaki.

To fully understand this concept, refer to "Conduit" entry in "Anunnaki Encyclopedia", volume one.

- **4-Code/Use according to mythology and esoterism:** Indoor, draw the geometrical symbol on the back of your favorite cooking pan. In a court of law, draw the symbol on a piece of paper and direct it toward the jury if applicable, otherwise, toward the judge.

- **5-Benefits:**
1-Improve health condition in general;
2-Bring justice to your cause.

- **6-Geometrical presentation/Symbol:** An eye inside a triangle.

***   ***   ***

9-Who Is Ahat?

The Answer

- **1-Origin:** Derived from the Phoenician Ahat and Aqhat.

- **2-Numerical value:** 77.

- **3-Meaning:** As defined in the "Anunnaki Encyclopedia"; Ahat was a Phoenician hero, a descendant from the Anunnaki, and a gift from god El to King Daniel who adopted him as his son.

Ahat was given a celestial bow made out of circular horns. Anat (A Syrian, Canaanite and Phoenician goddess of earth) was attracted to the bow, but Ahat refused to give her his bow. She got mad, and sent her attendant Yatpan, to kill Ahat. Ahat was killed, and his bow was lost during his struggle with Yaptan.

The gods became angry, cursed humans, and the supreme god Baal punished mankind by stopping the rains from falling on the lands of Phoenicia, thus creating a drought, and causing the crops to fail, and the stored grains to rot.

Ahat ascended to Ashtari (Planet Nibiru) and became a legion commander under his new Anunnaki's name "Aqhat", given to him by SinharMarduck.

- **4-Code/Use:** Early Phoenicians in Tyre, Sidon and Island of Arwad wrote Aqhat name on a piece of clay and buried underground each year before summer harvest.

According to Phoenician and Akkadian legends, this nourished the earth and protected grains and crops.

This sort of talisman can be used today for different purposes, such as creating new positive opportunities.

- **5-Benefits:**
1-Bringing good luck,
2- Increasing prosperity.

- **6-Geometrical presentation/Symbol:** A green leaf.

*** *** ***

10-Who Is Aa.Kim.LU? Was He The Creator And God Of The Anunnaki?

The Answer

Aa-kim-lU (Akimlu, AA.Kim.LU)

- **1-Origin:** Derived from the Anakh "Akim. LU".

- **2-Numerical value:** None. It is not allowed to assign a numerical value to his name.

- **3-Meaning:** It is the name of the creator of the Anunnaki, and seven galaxies according to "The Book of Rama-Dosh". Aa-kim-lu used "Rouh-D'ab-Sha.LIM" to create the Anunnaki, 7 billions years B.C.

- **4-Code/Use according to mythology and esoterism:** Strictly used during "Plasmic Manifestations".

- **5-Benefits:** Used for identification in the early stage of communications with superior beings.

- **6-Geometrical presentation/Symbol:** A spear with three bursting stars.

*** *** ***

71

11-What Is Al-A'kh?

The Answer

Al- A'kh (Al Hak)

- **1-Origin:** Derived from the Anakh AL. A'Kh.

- **2-Numerical value:** 1,100.

- **3-Meaning:** A system of administration and government based upon the Anunnaki social code. Later, Al-A'kh became an Arabic word for justice.

- **4-Code/Use according to mythology and esoterism:** Before you open your shop at the beginning of each month, write AL.A'Kh and the number 1,000 on the left side of the door of your shop. Write it with charcoal and wipe it at the end of the day before 6:00 PM.

- **5-Benefits:** It brings stability to your business.

- **6-Geometrical presentation/Symbol:**
  Two identical squares.

*** *** ***

12-What Is An?

The Answer

An

- **1-Origin:** Derived from the Anakh AN.

- **2-Numerical value:** 1,199.

- **3-Meaning:**
1-Source;
2-first breath;
3-first nourishment.
In Sumerian, it means celestial father. Commonly used by the Hurrians, Phoenicians, Elamites, Subarians, Sumerians, Medes, and Kasites.

- **4-Code/Use according to mythology and esoterism:** Write the word "An" and the name of your new-born child on the leaf of a white rose and keep it in a safe place for seven days.

- **5-Benefits:** It brings health and protection to newly born children.

- **6-Geometrical presentation/Symbol:** The letter "A" and a leaf of a white rose.

*** *** ***

13-Do Anunnaki Feel And React Like Us?

The Answer

There is a major misconception about the Anunnaki's emotions and the nature of their feelings.

Avalanches of erroneous theses were written about their cruelty, ferocious reptilian character, and particularly about abducting humans.

Among the most considerate extraterrestrial races are:

1-The Lyrans;
2-The Nordics;
3-The Anunnaki.

Unfortunately, misinformed writers, some of them are very well-known in the ufology community wrote chapters upon chapters describing how the Anunnaki and their remnants on earth control our mind and disrupt the order in our societies, because they have a malicious agenda. The truth is, the Anunnaki do not interfere in human affairs. They have left earth centuries ago. Those who are abducting humans are the "Grays".

The Anunnaki express their feelings just like we do. However, they do not shed tears, nor succumb to emotional crises. Their "sentimentality" is controlled by a "Conduit" directly linked to a community-collective-awareness. This means, that their emotions are regulated

– but not controlled – by an "intellect" channel. This channel is constantly balanced scientifically.

The female Anunnaki are more affectionate than their male counterparts.

For instance, at the Anunnaki Academy of Learning, male Anunnaki have developed the space-time travel, remote viewing and "cosmic projection" courses. Per contra, the female Anunnaki have developed arts and "social communication" study programs.

This comparison is self-explanatory. And if we go back in history, we discover that the genetically created men by male Anunnaki looked like robots and machines, while the final "product" of the early modern men as created by the female Annunaki had more appealing physical attributes, and more developed sense for aesthetics and artistic creativity.

Do The Anunnaki react and feel like us?

They do not react like humans, but they do express emotions and feelings.

Because their society is matriarchal in essence, the Anunnaki are deeply influenced by the female nature and element which translate into compassion, and devotion for their families.

Many of the Anunnaki look like us.

They share with humans many physical properties, and to a certain degree, a "partial" DNA!

*** *** ***

14-Who Was Gb'r (Angel Gabriel)?

The Answer

Angel Gabriel

- **1-Origin:** Derived from the Anakh Gb'r.

- **2-Numerical value:** Delta 1000.

- **3-Meaning:** An Anunnaki personage with mighty powers and major influence on the creation of the human race.

Angel Gabriel is not totally and exactly what the Judeo-Christian tradition portrays. The original name is "Gib-ra-il"; the guardian of Janat Adan or Edin (Garden of Eden), in Sumerian and in Anakh is Nin-il, or Nin-Lil. Gabriel is also called "Gab" and "Gab-r-il".

Gab means a female guardian, a governor or a protector. This explains why Angel Gabriel was represented to us as the guardian of the Garden of Eden. In the ancient texts of the Sumerians, Acadians and civilizations of the neighboring regions, "Gab-r" was the governor of "Janat Adan."

In various Semitic languages, "Janat" means paradise, and Eden is Idin or Adan. This is how we got Garden of Eden. Angel Gabriel, the Sumerian is more than a guardian, because he was called Nin-Ti which means verbatim: Life-Woman.

In other words, Angel Gabriel was three things:

1-Governor of the Garden of Eden;
2-A woman, NOT a man, because she was described as "the female who created life";
3-A geneticist who worked on the human DNA/creation of the human race. The word "Gab-r" was phonetically pronounced as: Gab'er.
The early Arabs adopted it as "Al Jaber" meaning many things including: force, authority, might, and governing. From "Al Jaber" important words, nouns and adjectives were derived. For instance, the word "Jabbar" means: mighty, powerful, capable, huge, giant, like the giants in the Bible and Sumerian/Anunnaki epics. "Jababira" is the plural of "Al Jabbar".

After the Arabs were converted to Islam, "Al Jaber" became "Al Jabbar"; one of the attributes and names of Allah (God).
In the Anakh (Anunnaki language), the word "Jabba-r-oout" means exactly the same thing in early Aramaic and modern Arabic: Authority, power, rule, reign.
It is obvious that the Anakh language deeply influenced Eastern and Western languages. One more surprise for the readers.
We find striking similarity in our Western vocabularies (Latin, Anglo-Saxon, French and Romance languages); Gab'r became gouverneur in French, governor in English, and gubernator in Latin.

The Sumerian Gabriel was also known under different names according to the Sumerian texts, such as "Nin-Hour-sagh", meaning the lady governess of the

88

mountain; an elevated region of the Garden of Eden. Gabriel "Gb'r", "Gab-Ril" as a female Anunnaki was the first to experiment with copies of a human, later to be called Adam.

But first, Gabriel created 7 different types of Homo Sapiens by using the DNA of primitive beings and the DNA of an Anunnaki. Gabriel's original creations were not very successful.

Later on, Gabriel used a most unexpected genetic source to create the final copy of the modern man. There are plenty of evidence and historical statements to prove this point. And all starts with her name "Nin-il", some times referred to as "Nin-ti".

In Anakh, Sumerian and Babylonian languages, the word "Ti" means "rib". In later versions of the ancient texts, "Nin-ti" became the "lady of the rib", also the "lady of life", and the "lady of creation".

Consequently, Adam, the man, was created from the rib of Gabriel, the female Anunnaki; the "lady of the rib". This contradicts the story of the creation of Adam and Eve as told in the Judeo-Christian tradition. According to the Sumerians and the Anakh, a woman created man; it was NOT a man who created a woman (Eve).

And the female Anunnaki (Gabriel) used her rib to create Adam.

The early translators - and possibly, intentionally misleading scribes and usurpers of the truth - of the ancient texts and epics of Sumer got it wrong, and their fake story of the creation of Adam and Eve invaded the Hebraic, Christian and Islamic holy scriptures.

- **4-Code/Use:** Write the word "Gb'r" seven times on a water cup and drink it in three steps.

- **5-Benefits:** It eliminates shoulder pains caused by fatigue and office work.

- **6-Geometrical presentation/Symbol:** The letter "V".

*** *** ***

15-What Is Bab (Ba'ab)?
Is It The Anunnaki Star Gate?

The Answer

Bab (Ba'ab):

- **1-Origin:** Derived from the Anakh Ba'ab.

- **2-Numerical value:** 700

- **3-Meaning:** An Anunnaki's stargate, from which an Anunnaki earth remnant leaves earth to reach Nibiru.

The Bab opens only from the earth side and closes behind the traveling Anunnaki. It means door in several Middle Eastern and Anatolian languages, including Arabic and Turkish with identical pronunciation.

- **4-Code/Use according to mythology and esoterism:** Write the words "Bab" in capital letters on the frame of a window in your house.

- **5-Benefits:** It rejuvenates positive energy inside your home.

- **6-Geometrical presentation/Symbol:**
  Two parallel triangles.

*** *** ***

16-What Is Fik'r?
Is It Mind Or Soul?

The Answer

Fik'r:

- **1-Origin:** Derived from the Anakh Fik-R'r, and Fik.Ra.Sa. The esoteric Arabic word "Firasa" is derived from Fik.Ra.Sa. It means in Arabic the ability to read thoughts, understand the psyche of a person just by looking at him/her.

The Ulema used Fik'r to read the mind, learn about the intentions of others, and assess the level of intelligence of people. Almost all rulers in ancient Persia, Phoenicia and later in Egypt employed in their royal courts, "People of Firasa".

They consulted with them during visits of dignitaries and officials from foreign countries. It was the secret science of learning about the personality of people through the study of physiognomy.

This science was called "Firasa". One of the greatest Ulema masters and experts in the field was Fakher Addīn Al- Rāzī.

His noted treatise on Firasa; The Science of psycho-physiognomy was inspired by the teachings of the Ulema. In the unpublished original edition of his treatise, several Anunnaki syllables and geometric forms were included in "Al Moukamma" the introduction of the book dedicated to the "true believers of the higher knowledge".

- **2-Numerical value:** Aleph 7.

97

- **3-Meaning:** As defined in the "Anunnaki Encyclopedia"; Soul is an invention of early humans who needed to believe in a next life.

It was through the soul that mortals could and would hope to continue to live after death. Soul as an element or a substance does not exist anywhere inside the human body. Instead, there is a non-physical substance called "Fik'r" that makes the brain function, and it is the brain that keeps the body working, not the soul.

The "Fik'r" was the primordial element used by the Anunnaki at the time they created the final form of the human race. Fik'r was NOT used in the early seven prototypes of the creation of mankind according to the Sumerian texts.

The "Fik'r", although it is the primordial source of life for our physical body, it is not to be considered as DNA, because DNA is a part of "Fik'r"; DNA is the physical description of our genes, a sort of a series of formulas, numbers and sequences of what there in our body, the data and history of our genes, genetic origin, ethnicity, race, so on.

Consider "Fik'r" as a cosmic-sub-atomic-intellectual-extraterrestrial (Meaning non-physical, non-earthy) depot of all what it constituted, constitutes and shall continue to constitute everything about you. And it is infinitesimally small.

But it can expand to an imaginable dimension, size and proportions. It stays alive and continues to grow after we pass away if it is still linked to the origin of its creation, in our case the Anunnaki. The "Fik'r" is linked to the Anunnaki our creators through a "Conduit" found in the cells of the brain. For now, consider "Fik'r" as a small molecule, a bubble.

- **4-Code/Use according to mythology and esoterism:** It is the most important vehicle for the mind "intellect". Through Fik'r, a person can enter higher dimensions.

- **5-Benefits:** It is of a major importance to train your Fik'r. "Transmission of the mind" training sessions can develop extra-sensorial faculties and open your "inner eye" commonly referred to as the "Third Eye".

*** *** ***

17-What Is An-Hayya'h? Is It The Original Source Of Life?

The Answer

- **1-Origin:** Derived from the Anakh A.Ha.YA

- **2-Numerical value:** 1111, also Al-Lef 111.

- **3-Meaning:** As defined in the "Anunnaki Encyclopedia"; "An-Hayya'h" could be the most important word in the whole literature of the Anunnaki Anakh, and Ulema, as well as in the written history of humanity, because it deals with:

1-Origin of man on earth;
2-How humans are connected to the Anunnaki;
3-Importance of water vis-à-vis humans and Anunnaki;
4-The life of humans;
5-Proof that it was the "Woman" who created man, Adam and the human race via her Anunnaki identity;
6-The return of the Anunnaki to earth;
7-Humanity salvation, hopes, and a better future for all of us; a gift from our ancestors and creators, the Anunnaki.
I will try to explain the whole concept as clear as possible, because it is extremely difficult to find the proper and accurate word or words in our terrestrial languages and vocabularies.

The word "An-Hayya'h" is composed of:
1-"An" or "A" (Pronounced Aa), or "Aelef
"(Pronounced A'lef).
It is the same letter in Anakh, Akkadian, Canaanite,
Babylonian, Assyrian, Ugaritic, Phoenician, Moabite,
Siloam, Samaritan, Lachish, Hebrew, Aramaic,
Nabataean Aramaic, Syriac, and Arabic.
All these languages are derived from the Anakh. (Note:
The early Greeks adopted the Phoenician Alphabet, and
the Latin and Cyrillic came from the Greek.
The Hebrew, Aramaic and Greek scripts all came from
the Phoenician. Arabic and most of Indian scriptures
came from the Aramaic.
The entire Western world received its languages from
the Phoenicians, the descendants of the Anunnaki).
"An" in Anakh (Anunnaki language), means one of the
following:

- 1-Beginning;
- 2-The very first;
- 3-The ultimate;
- 4-The origin;
- 5-Water.

On Earth, this word became "Alef" in Phoenician,
Aramaic, Hebrew, Syriac and Arabic.
Alef is the beginning of the alphabet in these languages.
In Latin, it's "A" and in Greek is "Alpha". In Hebrew,
the "Aleph" consists of two yuds (Pronounced Yood);
one yud is situated to the upper right and the other yud to
the lower left. Both yuds are joined by a diagonal *vav*.
They represent the higher water and the lower water, and
between them the heaven.
This mystic-kabalistic interpretation was given to us by
Rabbi Isaac Louria. Water is extremely important in all

104

the sacred scriptures, as well as in the vast literature and scripts of extraterrestrials and Anunnaki.

Water links humans to the Anunnaki. In the Babylonian account of the Creation, Tablet 1 illustrates Apsu (male), representing the primeval fresh water, and Tiamat (female), the primeval salt water.

In the Torah, the word "water" was mentioned in the first day of the creation of the world: "And the spirit of God hovered over the surface of the water." In the Chassidut, the higher water is "wet" and "warm", and represents the closeness to Yahweh (God), and it brings happiness to man. The lower water is "cold", and brings unhappiness because it separates us from Yahweh (God), and man feels lonely and abandoned.

The Ten Commandments commences with the letter "Alef": "Anochi (I) am God your God who has taken you out of the land of Egypt, out of the house of bondage."

The letter "Alef" holds the secret of man, its creation and the whole universe (Midrash). In Hebrew, the numeric value of "Aleph" is 1. And the meaning is:

- 1-First;
- 2-Adonai;
- 3-Leader;
- 4-Strength;
- 5-Ox;
- 6-Bull,
- 7-Thousand;
- 8-To teach.

According to Jewish teaching, each Hebrew letter is a spiritual force and power by itself, and comes directly from Yahweh (God).

This force contains the raw material for the creation of the world and man. The Word of God ranges from the Aleph (the very first letter) to the Tav (the last letter) in Hebrew. In Revelation 1:8, Jesus said: "I am Alpha and Omega, the beginning and the ending."

In John 1:1-3, as the Word becomes Jesus, the Lord Jesus is also the Aleph and the Tav, as well as the Alpha and the Omega. In Him exists all the forces, and spiritual powers of the creation. Jesus is also connected to water, an essential substance for the purification of the body and the soul, this is why Christians got to be baptized in water.

In Islam, water is primordial and considered as the major force of the creation of the universe.

The Prophet Mohammad said (From the Quran): "Wa Khalaknah Lakoum min al Ma'i, koula chay en hay", meaning: And WE (Allah) have created for you from water everything alive." The Islamic numeric value of Aleph and God is 1.

To the Anunnaki and many extraterrestrial civilizations, the "An" or "Alef" represents number 1, also Nibiru, the constellation Orion, the star Aldebaran, and above all the female aspect of the creation symbolized in an Anunnaki woman "Gb'r" (Angel Gabriel to us) have the humeric value of 1.

2-Hayya'h (Also A-haYA, Aelef-hayat) means:
- a-Life;
- b-Creation;
- c-Humans;
- d-Earth, where the first human (female human was the first created human on earth) was created.

106

In Arabic, Hebrew, Aramaic, Turkish, Syriac, and so many Eastern languages, the Anunnaki words "Hayya'h" and "Hayat" mean the same thing: Life. Quite astonishing!

But the most striking part of our story is that the original name of Eve is not Eve, but "Hawwa" derived directly from Hayya. How do we know this?

Very simple: Eve's name in the Bible is "Hawwa", also "Chevvah". In the Quran is also "Hawwa", and in every single Semitic and Akkadian script, Eve is called Hawwa or Hayat, meaning the giver of life; the source of the creation.

Now, if we combine the 2 words: An +Hayya'h or Hayat, we get this: Beginning; The very first; The ultimate; The origin; Water + Life; Creation; Humans; Earth, where the first was created; Woman. And the whole meaning becomes: The origin of the creation and first thing or person who created the life of humans was a woman (Eve; Hawwa) or water.

Amazingly enough, in Anakh, woman and water mean the same thing, because woman represents water according to the Babylonian, Sumerians and Anunnaki tablets, as clearly written in the Babylonian-Sumerian account of the Creation, Tablet 1.

And I have more surprises to share with you: The Anunnaki who created us genetically some 65,000 B.C. lived on earth with us, in Iraq (Sumer, Mesopotamia, Babylon) and Lebanon (Loubnan, Pheonicia, Phinikia).

They taught our ancestors how to write, how to speak, how to play music, how to build temples, how to navigate, as well as geometry, algebra, metallurgy, irrigation, astronomy, you name it. But the human races disappointed them, for the early human beings were cruel, violent, greedy and ungrateful. So, the Anunnaki gave up on us and left earth.

The few remaining Anunnaki living in Iraq and Lebanon were killed by savage military legions from Greece, Turkey and other nations of the region. The Anunnaki left earth for good.

Other extraterrestrial races came to earth, but these celestial visitors were not friendly and considerate like our ancestors the Anunnaki.

The new extraterrestrials had a different plan for humanity, and their agenda included abduction of women and children, animal mutilation, genetic experiments on human beings, creating a new hybrid race, etc…

The Anunnaki did not totally forget us. After all, many of their women were married to humans, and many of our women were married to Anunnaki. Ancient history, the Bible, Sumerian Texts, Babylonian scriptures, Phoenician tablets, and historical accounts from around the globe recorded these events.

You can find them, almost intact, in archeological sites in Iraq and Lebanon, as well as in museums, particularly the British Museum, the Iraqi Museum and the Lebanese Museum. So, before leaving us, the Anunnaki activated in our cells the infinitesimally invisible multi-multi-microscopic gene of An-Hayya'h. It was implanted in our organism and became a vital composition of our DNA.

Humans are not yet aware of this, as we were not aware of the existence of our DNA for thousands of years.

As our medicine, science and technology advance, we will be able one day to discover that miniscule, invisible, undetectable An-Hayya'h, exactly as we have discovered our DNA. An-Hayya'h cannot be detected yet in our laboratories.

It is way beyond our reach and our comprehension. It is extremely powerful, because it is the very source of our existence.

Through An-Hayya'h, the Anunnaki remained in touch with us, even though we are not aware of it. It is linked directly to a "Conduit" and to a "Miraya" (Monitor, or mirror) on Nibiru. Every single human being on the face of the earth is linked to the outer-world of the Anunnaki through An-Hayya'h. And it is faster than the speed of light.

It reaches the Anunnaki through "Babs" (Star gates). For now, we will call it "molecule" or "bubble".

This molecule travels the universe and reaches the "Miraya" of the Anunnaki through a "Conduit" integrated in our genes and our brain cells by the Anunnaki some 65,000 years ago.

But what is a "Conduit"?

I will explain below.

Does every human possess a "conduit"? The answer is yes.

All humans have a "Conduit" just like the Anunnaki, because it is part of our DNA.

It is impossible to explain how a "Conduit" works inside the human brain, and/or how it works for a human being. I will explain it in the Anunnaki's context. The creation of the "Conduit" is the most important procedure done for each Anunnaki student on the first day of his or her entrance into the Academy. A new identity is created for each Anunnaki student by the development of a new pathway in his or her mind, connecting the student to the rest of the Anunnaki's psyche.

Simultaneously, the cells check with the "other copy" of the mind and body of the Anunnaki student, to make sure that the "Double" and "Other Copy" of the Mind and body of the student are totally clean.

During this phase, the Anunnaki student temporarily loses his or her memory, for a very short time. This is how the telepathic faculty is developed, or enhanced in everyone.

It is necessary, since to serve the total community of the Anunnaki, the individual program inside each Anunnaki student is immediately shared with everybody.

The Anunnaki have collective intelligence and individual intelligence. And this is directly connected to two things: the first is the access to the "Community Depot of Knowledge" that any Anunnaki can tap in and update and acquire additional knowledge.

The second is an "individual Prevention Shield," also referred to as "Personal Privacy." This means that an Anunnaki can switch on and off his/her direct link, or perhaps better defined as a channel, to other Anunnaki. By establishing the "Screen" or "Filter" an Anunnaki can block others from either communication with him or her, or simply prevent others from reading any personal thought.

"Filter" "Screen" and "Shield" are interchangeably used to describe the privacy protection.

In addition, an Anunnaki can program telepathy and set it up on chosen channels, exactly as we turn on our radio set and select the station we wish to listen to. Telepathy has several frequency, channels and stations. When the establishment of the Conduit is complete, the student leaves the conic cell, where the procedure has taken place, and heads to the classroom.

Now, the second question is: How does an Anunnaki receive the content of a "Conduit" to allow him/her to watch over us?

The Anunnaki created the "Conduit", the "Miraya" and the "An-Hayya'h" to watch over us, even though we do not deserve it.

The Anunnaki have been watching us, monitoring our activities, listening to our voices, witnessing our wars, brutality, greed and indifference toward each others for centuries. But they did not interfere. But now, they will, because they fear two things that could destroy earth and annihilate the human race:

1-The domination of earth and the human race by the Greys;

2-The destruction of human life and planet Earth on the hands of humans.

The whole earth could blow up. Should this happen, the whole solar system could be destroyed. For we know, should anything happen to the Moon, the earth will cease to exist. This is an absolute truth and a fact accepted by all scientists. "An-Hayya'h" is our umbilical cord, our birth cord that attaches us to the Anunnaki.

No matter how silly and crazy this concept might look to many of us, one day, we will accept and possibly we might understand its mind-boggling mysteries, when our science, technology and mind explore wider dimensions, and reach a higher level of cosmic awareness and intelligence.

But this is not the whole story about An-Hayya'h; the most delightful and comforting aspect of it, is the hope, peace, a brighter future, and a better life we can accomplish and reach when we discover how to use it without abusing it.

Every one of us can do that. If in your lifespan, you remain unable to attain these results, your An-Hayya'h will always be there for you to use before you depart this earth.

It will never go away, because it is part of you. Without it you couldn't exist. Just before you die, your brain out of the blue wills active it for you.

Seconds before you leave earth (Not your body, not your soul) your mind will project the reenactment of all the events and acts (bad and good) in your life, past, present and future, and "zoom" you right toward your next nonphysical destination, where and when you judge yourself, your deeds, your existence and decide whether you wish to elevate yourself to a higher dimension, or stay in the state of nothingness and loneliness. No, you will not return to earth, nor your soul will migrate to another soul or another body, because the Anunnaki do not believe in reincarnation or a return to earth.

Earth is the lowest sphere of existence for humans. Thus, you are always connected to the Anunnaki in this life and the next one.

- **4-Code/Use according to mythology and esoterism:** Because it is the source of life, An-Hayya'h as a word entered the sacred language of the "Intellect" and communication medium of the enlightened teachers.

It was pronounced 7 times at the beginning of each "Ij-Ti.Mah" (Reunion) of the elders. Some believe that the first letter of this word "Heh", not An, had supernatural healing powers. Talismans were created to hold the "Heh". The Templars of the Island of Malta honored it and engraved on their swords. The Phoenician-Jewish-Aramaic-Arabic "Heh" if illustrated as two letters, it creates the shape of an esoteric rose. And the rose was the early secret and esoteric symbol of many secret learned societies, and Crusaders who were searching for the Philosophical Stone in Palestine.

- **5-Benefits:** No pragmatic visible application. However, it could facilitate negotiations between sympathizers of the occult and practitioners of "Al Sihr".

The legendary alchemist Nicholas Flamel used it in many of his metal transmutations formulas. Allegedly, the letter "Heh" was found on a measuring tape retrieved at the UFO crash site in Roswell. If you join the two ends of the letter, you get the sign of infinity. You can do that just by drawing a straight line between the top and bottom of the letter.

Many historians believed for centuries, that the infinity sign was a Greek symbol. The truth is, the infinity sign is a numerical form for 2 parallel words. The Ulema used it as a mental stimulus for extraterrestrial entities plasmic apparitions.

According to the Book of Rama-Dosh, the converted "Heh" letter...in the possession of an honorable person creates wealth, and opportunities for prosperity. In tarot, the magician begins to work under the sign of infinity.

Using the infinity sign, the magician of the Tarot make financial difficulties disappear. If you draw the "HEH" twice side by side on a candle, you will increase your chances of financial success.

It appears as a ridiculous story for the rational person, and I totally agree. Ironically, 3 out 4 "scientific" persons I knew and who ridiculed the whole idea, tried it at least once.

*** *** ***

18-What Is Ar. Hal? Is It Going Back In Time?

The Answer

- **1-Origin:** Derived from the Anak'h word Aa. R'Hal.Ra

- **2-Numerical value:** 888

- **3-Meaning:** This is a very difficult phenomenon to comprehend.

To understand the concept, the closest metaphor in human terms would be that if you wish you could do something differently, change the past, change a life decision, like perhaps, going back in time to a point before you have made a bad decision.

Or, if you think that you could do some good if you could change an entire event. In the Anunnaki's case, they have the solutions for these dilemmas. An Anunnaki can split himself/herself in two, or more if necessary, and move on to a universe that is very much like the one they live on (Nibiru).

There are so many universes, and some of them do not resemble Nibiru at all.

If an Anunnaki wishes to branch out and move on, he/she must study the matter very carefully and make the right selection.

And the branching, or splitting, results in exact copies of the person of the Anunnaki, both physically and mentally.

117

At the moment of separation, each separate individual copy of an Anunnaki grows, mentally, in a different direction, follows his or her own free will and decisions, and eventually the two are not exactly alike. So what do they do, first of all?

The old one stays where he/she is and follows his/her old patterns as he/she wishes.

The new one might land one minute, or a month, or a year, before the decision he/she wants to change or avoid. Let's take this scenario for instance; Some 30,000 years ago in his life-span; an Anunnaki male was living a nice life with his wife and family. But he felt that he did not accomplish much, and suddenly he wanted to be more active in the development of the universe; a change caused by witnessing a horrendous event such as a certain group of beings in his galaxy destroying an entire civilization, and killing millions of the inhabitants, in order to take over their planet for various purposes.

It happened while an Anunnaki was on a trip, and he actually saw the destruction and actions of war while he was traveling.

It was quite traumatic, and he thought, at that moment, that he must be active in preventing such events from occurring again, ever.

So, he went back in time to be in a spot to prevent these fateful events from happening again. There, in that new dimension, the Anunnaki leaves his former self (A copy of himself) as a guardian and a protector. The other copy (Perhaps one of the original ones) is still on Nibiru.

- **4-Code/Use according to mythology and esoterism:** There is no connection to mythology and esoterim.

118

The "Branching Out" phenomenon occurred in one of the designated locals of the Anunnaki Hall of Records, also called in terrestrial term "Akashic Records."

- **5-Benefits:** The possibility of visiting other worlds, dimensions and civilizations.

- **6-Geometrical presentation/Symbol:**
  Not applicable

*** *** ***

19-Do Anunnaki Have Social Classes?

The Answer

The Anunnaki's society is divided into two classes: The lower class and the higher class. Both are under the control of a "Sinhar" or a "Baalshalimroot-An'kgh." Baalshalimroot-An'kgh means: Greatest Leader.
Sinhar means: Leader or Ruler.
When the word "Sinhar" is attached to "Mardack" or "Marduck", the new meaning becomes: Leader of the Ultimate Energy.
Why "Ultimate Energy" is so important?
Because the Anunnaki do not believe in the God we know and worship.
To the Anunnaki, the universe was NOT created by God. The universe is "What It Is" or "Creation by Itself".
It gets more and more complicated when we try to understand the psyche of the Anunnaki, and how this psyche defines the elements of the universe in a very strange and complicated language.
Consequently, trying to fully understand their language using our terrestrial vocabulary and perception of life is a fruitless effort.

There is nothing metaphysical to it.
It is simply a scientific lexicon our mind cannot grasp.
History has taught us, that as the level of knowledge reaches a higher standard, and technology advances, language changes and new terminology is automatically added to our lexicon and expressions.

123

The same principle applies to the language of the Anunnaki which reflects an extremely advanced level of technology.

And this is the reason behind our inability to understand their language, and how they describe the universe. Let's for now, forget about all these semantics and galactic jargon, and return to the Anunnaki's social classes:

- **1**-The lower class of the Anunnaki consists of the Nephilim.
- **2**-The higher class of the Anunnaki consists of the Sinhar-Harib.
- **3**-Baalshalimroot-An'kgh is the Anunnaki's greatest leader. He rules both classes. His name means the following:

- **a**-Baal: God; Creator; the Leading Force of creation;
- **b**-Shalim: Friendly Greetings; Message of the Leader; Peace; Root: The Way; Direction of Victory;
- **c**-An'kgh: Eternity; Wisdom; Eye of Great Knowledge; the Infinite; the Ever-Lasting Energy.

The second in command is Adoun Rou'h Dar, also Adon-Nefs-Beyth. His name means the following:

- **a**-Adoun or Adon: The Lord; God; The Ultimate One;
- **b**-Rou'h or Nefs: The Spirit; The Original Creative Force; the Soul; the Mind;
- **c**-Dar, Beit or Beyth: Residence; the House of the Lord. Members of the higher class of the Anunnaki are 9 foot tall. Their lifespan averages 350,000-400,000 years.

The Igigi did co-exist with the Anunnaki, and shared some traits with them, but they were totally dissimilar in their physical shape, and had different intentions as far as the human race was concerned.

The Igigi are 245 million years older than the Anunnaki. Scholars like Sitchin and Gardner have equated the Anunnaki with the Nephilim.

This is not totally correct.

The lower class of the Anunnaki are the Nephilim, although many historians call them sometimes Anakim or Elohim.

The higher class of the Anunnaki is ruled by Baalshalimroot, and his followers or subjects are called the "Shtaroout-Hxall Ain", meaning the inhabitants of the house of knowledge, or "those who see clearly." Ain: The word "Ain" was later adopted by the early inhabitants of the Arab Peninsula. "Ain" in Arabic means "eye".

In the secret teachings of Sufism, visions of Al Hallaj, and of the greatest poetess of Sufism, Rabiha' Al Adawi Yah, known also as "Ha Chi katou Al Houbb Al Ilahi" (The mistress of the divine love), and in the banned book *Shams Al Maa'Ref Al Kubrah* (Book of the Sun of the Great Knowledge), the word "eye" meant the ultimate knowledge, or wisdom from above.

"Above" clearly indicates the heavens. Later on, it was used to symbolize the justice of God or "God watching over us." And much later in history, several societies and cultures adopted the "eye" as an institutional symbol and caused it to appear on many temples' pillars, bank notes, money bills, and religious texts.

Eye of the Anunnaki

Freemasons and Illuminati favorite symbol is the Anunnaki's eye. And as everything changes in time and takes on different forms and meanings, the 'eye' became a 'triangle,' a very secretive and powerful symbol. George Washington carried this triangle with him wherever he went, and wore it during official ceremonies. If you double and reverse the triangle, you get the Star of David.

This very triangle is visible on many extraterrestrial spacecrafts and on uniforms of military personnel in secret American military bases underground, working on alien technology and propulsion systems.

The triangle became the insignia of the New World Order.

On February 17, 1,953, an American millionaire by the name of Paul Warburg who was involved with secret organizations and the Freemasons in Virginia and Washington, DC, shouted before the Senate of the United States of America: "We shall have world government whether or not you like it, by conquest or consent."

The 'Triangle' can be a negative force. When integrated without balance and cosmic harmony.

In other words, used without spatial equilibrium, in architectural design and lined up on territories' maps, the triangle becomes a negative force on the map. If the three sides of the triangle are separated, such separation can cause serious health problems.

The triangle becomes three lines of negative energy. This energy is not easily detected; nevertheless it runs strong and deep underground.

People who live above these lines suffer enormously.

In many instances, this negative power or current can negatively affect the present and future of many human beings.

Similar to some Ufologists who can identify UFOs' hot spots on earth, usually above ground, descendants of the extraterrestrials can identify and locate the negative currents underground. Each country has these negative currents or circuits underground. I do not wish to scare my readers, but I must inform you that some American states are located above these lines. For example, Mississippi, Alabama, the northern part of Washington, DC, and two areas in Brooklyn, New York share this misfortune.

20-Do Anunnaki Believe In "God?

The Answer

Anunnaki's god is not the same "God" we worship on Earth.

The grand leader of the Anunnaki (Called the creator of energy), and other Anunnaki kings and commanders of the first three expeditions to earth were worshiped by the early human races as gods. The Anunnaki do not believe in a God in the same way we do, even though they were the ones who created and originated the early forms of all our religions on earth. However, those Anunnaki who brought religion to earth were of a lower class of the Anakh (Anunnaki).

The god (Yah-Weh) they brought to earth and planted in the mind of primitive humans, was a vengeful and terrifying god; a fact the Gnostics and early scholars of the Coptic Church in Egypt were fully aware of.

Their doctrines show their disdain for such a god, and consequently, they called him the 'Creator of Evil and Darkness.'

Later on in history, the Gnostics began to spread the word that this earth was not created by the God of the Church, but rather by an evil demi-god.

The more advanced human beings who interacted with the Anunnaki shared similar beliefs.

Today, if humans would learn about all this, the religious aspect of our beliefs would be most difficult to reconcile.

Members of an early Anunnaki expedition to Phoenicia taught the Phoenicians how to develop their language, and revealed to them the secret powerful names and attributes of Baalshalimroot.

They instructed them not to use these words for ill purposes. Particularly, the word 'Baalazamhour-Il' is never to be pronounced or written.

Later on in history, the Habiru (Hebrew) religiously observed this instruction, and thus, pronouncing the name of God became forbidden in Jewish tradition.

However, the Anunnaki did reveal to the Phoenicians and Sumerians seven positive and powerful names/attributes of the Grand Leader (Call him God in terrestrial terms).

If well used, these words can bring prosperity, good health, and salvation in moments of difficulty and despair.

The prophet Mohammad learned these seven words from an early Christian ascetic, a Sahara hermit called Raheb Bouhayra.

Today, Muslims all over the world are aware of these seven words or names. They call them in written Arabic 'Asma' Al Lah Al Sabha' Al Housna,' meaning the seven lovely names of God.

These names do not have numerical value or secret meanings as many scholars claim, simply because they were not originally written in a geometrical form, and did not correspond to a "true god".

(Note: None of these words appeared on the alleged hieroglyphic measuring tape that the Americans found at the UFO crash site in Roswell.

The symbols and geometrical signs Americans found in Roswell were biochemical symbols.)

Also, early names of the Hebrew God were of an extraterrestrial origin. It is true that the ancient Sumerian texts and records mentioned names of some of the Anunnaki leaders such as Utu, Ningishzida, Ninki, Marduk, Enki, Enlil, Inanna, but the greatest name of all was Baalshalimroot, also referred to as "Baalshalimroot-An'kgh." He was not depicted by the Anunnaki as a god. Terah, the father of Abraham, mistakenly worshiped Baalshalimroot-An'kgh as "God".

Early Semites made the same mistake when they worshiped the leaders of the Anunnaki as gods, later to be called Bene Ha-Elohim, meaning the children of the gods. The Anunnaki never introduced themselves as gods.

The Jewish words "El Elyon" and "Yahweh" (Jehovah) were taken directly from the Anunnaki's written language. The original word was "Yah'weh-El' Ankh" and El Elyon was "Il Ilayon-imroot."

Some scholars equated the Anunnaki with the Nephilim. This is not totally correct. The lower class of the Anunnaki are the Nephilim, although many historians call them sometimes Ana-KIm or Elohim.

Elohim was interpreted by the early human race including the Hebrew as "GOD" or "My Lord". Elohim is the plural of Eli.

And Eli became "god" in many Semitic languages, including Hebrew and Aramaic.

133

It has the same meaning in Aramaic, Hebrew, Phoenician, Akkadian and Arabic. And it was frequently used in reference to God. Even Jesus Christ used it. On the cross, Jesus said in Aramaic: "Eli, Eli, Lama Shabaktani", meaning: "My God, my God, why hast thou forsaken me?

The higher class of the Anunnaki (RafaaTH) is ruled by Baalshalimroot, and his followers or subjects are called the 'Shtaroout-Hxall Ain,' meaning the inhabitants of the house of knowledge, (Mistakenly, the Aramaic and Hebrew texts refer to as: House of God) or 'those who see clearly. At one point in ancient times, the Anunnaki told the Phoenicians that there is no god (One God) ruling over the entire universe.

However, the high priest of Melkart (Chief god in Tyre, Carthage and many regions in the Near and Middle East) instructed the temple's priests to mislead the people, and spread the word that the Anunnaki were celestial gods visiting earth and were constantly working with the Phoenician gods

In the early tales about Kadmos (Kadmus), the Phoenician prince who lived around 2,000 B.C. according to Herodotus of Halicarnassus (482-B.C.-426 B.C.), the concept of one god instead of many gods began to surface.

It was based upon the belief that the Anunnaki followed one supreme leader who created the entire human race. But even then, the term "god" did not mean the "God" we worship today.

Kadmos was the first Phoenician scholar and thinker who knew that "God" did not create mankind, and that the universe was not created by the supreme god or gods of the Phoenicians, the neighboring Near Eastern civilizations or the Anunnaki. Kadmos was and still is one of the brightest minds in the history of humanity; he was recognized by the ancient Greeks (Hellenes) as the creator of the Alphabet.

Kadmos founded the legendary city of Thebes and built the first acropolis in ancient Greece. The Greeks called him Kadmos, and to honor him, they called the city of Thebes "Kademeia" (From Kadmos) after him. Many words and letters from the Phoenician alphabet derived from the Anunnaki language (Anak'h).

Kadmos wrote down its final format according to the instructions of the Anunnaki. So, he knew what he was talking about; he knew from the Anunnaki that there is no such thing as one god (Judeo-Christian God) who created Adam, Eve, and all of us, because he was one of their students.

***   ***   ***

21-Where Did The Anunnaki Create Their First Colonies On Earth?

The Answer

Where Did The Anunnaki Create Their First Colonies On Earth?

449.000 years ago, under the leadership of Enki, the Anunnaki landed on Earth. The Anunnaki established their first colonies on the lands surrounding Phoenicia, Syria and Iraq. But their first cities and housing facilities were erected near Baalbeck, followed by Eridu. The Anunnaki used a sort of laser beams-anti-gravity tools to lift and transport enormous stones exceeding 1,500 tones each to build their first labs, landing and launching pads and to strengthen their gold mines.

- Their operations extended to regions neighboring Iran, Jordan and Israel.
- Years later, they concentrated their mining projects in Sumer, where they built enormous cities. However, during their first expedition, the Anunnaki did not relinquish the colonies they established in Phoenicia (Baalbeck and Tyre).
- The first Anunnaki's expedition included a multitude of scientists, topographers, ecologists, irrigation experts, engineers, architects, metallurgists, mineralogists, and military men.
- The objectives and purposes of this expedition were not exclusively gold mining and the

extraction of rich minerals from earth's oceans and seas.

However, assessing the natural resources and enormous wealth of earth in minerals and gold, the Anunnaki quickly realized that they needed a larger man-power; something they did not anticipate.

Thus, it became necessary to bring more Anunnaki to Earth. Consequently, more landings were en route. And gold mining became the Anunnaki new quest.

*** *** ***

22-Are The Anunnaki Immortal?

The Answer

Are The Anunnaki Immortal?

Immortality is a concept created by the human race. And because it is understood and measured by time and duration, this concept is no longer a reality. For we know that time becomes irrelevant or non-existent beyond our solar system. On aliens' planets, time and space as two separated things or two separate "plans" do not exist. The M theory as well as the parallel universe and multiple universes theories can explain this phenomenon to a certain degree.

- So, if there is no time per se, by itself, the notion or concept of immortality is not applicable.
- The Anunnaki do not think like us. They don't define immortality as we do, because they do not equate immortality with duration or with "Time".
- No, the Anunnaki don't believe in immortality, even though they can live up to 400,000 years. Is there an after-life once those 450,000 years come to an end?
- Yes. The Anunnaki calculate, plan and duplicate everything, All Anunnaki have a double; they reproduce themselves while alive.

- It means, they create copies of themselves and store those copies.
- These copies retain everything including memory. And they can repeat this process for ever.

However, there is a limit. And this occurs when the last bio-cell is no longer strong enough to create the energy needed to keep the mind functioning and the body's organs working perfectly.

*** *** ***

23-Do The Anunnaki Speak Or Understand Our Languages?

The Answer

Do The Anunnaki Speak Or Understand Our Languages?

Languages on Earth:
All our spoken languages derived directly from extraterrestrial languages. And all terrestrial languages derived from the Phoenician Alphabet. Many of the Phoenician linguists and early creators of their Alphabet borrowed numerous words and expressions from the higher class of the Anunnaki. Ancient Phoenician texts and poems, recorded on tablets found in Tyre, Sidon, Ugarit, Amrit, and the Island of Arwad included reference to symbols and words taken from the written language of the upper class of the Anunnaki.

The first genetically created race could not speak, and the concept of language was completely unknown to humans. Thousands of years later, the Anunnaki taught the new race of humans how to speak, read, and write. Members of an early Anunnaki expedition to Phoenicia taught the Phoenicians how to create their language, and revealed to them the secret powerful names and attributes of Baalshalimroot.

They instructed them not to use these words for ill purposes. Particularly, the word "Baalazamhour-Il" is never to be said, spelled, or written. Later on in history, the Hebrews religiously observed this instruction, and pronouncing the word of name of God became forbidden.

The language of the Anunnaki was taught to the early Phoenicians who lived in the ancient cities of Tyre, Sidon, Byblos, Afka and Batroun. Phoenicia borrowed her Alphabet from the Anunnaki.

The 7 powerful names and attributes of the Anunnaki's grand leader were given to the early Phoenicians in a ritual ceremony in Tyre

Yes, extraterrestrials are capable of speaking and understanding many languages, including our own.

They assimilate and "compute" words and sentences with mathematical formulas and numerical values. Some extraterrestrials have limited vocal chords capabilities, but they can very quickly acquire additional vocal faculties by rewinding sounds and vibes.

Contrary to what many contactees and others said, extraterrestrials from higher dimensions do not talk like computerized machines.

They have their own language but also they can absorb and assimilate all the languages on earth in a blink of an eye via the reception and emission of a "spatial memory."

At first, the voice of an alien from a higher dimension sounds like an old record that was played at the wrong speed – fast, squeaky, scratching. Then the sound adjusts itself, and the voice becomes a normal human voice. A very pleasant human voice.

Many of the Anunnaki's letters cannot be pronounced by Westerners because of the limitation of their vocal chords.

Anunnaki's language used by Americans:

The American top military scientists who work in secret military bases and aliens' laboratories on earth have an extraterrestrial lexicon, and use it constantly.

In that lexicon, or dictionary, you will find variations of Phoenician and Sumerian symbols.

Some letters represent maritime and celestial symbols and measurements.

The fact that the Americans are still using this extraterrestrial language should be enough to convince you that the US deals with extraterrestrials, and Zeta Reticuli descendants, live among us, otherwise why would anyone learn a language that cannot be used to communicate with people who speak it and write it?

On some of the manifestos of military parts used in anti-gravity secret laboratories underground in the United States, several letters were borrowed from the "Enuma Elish" of Sumeria and regularly appeared on the top right corner of each document. In the eighties, those Sumerian numbers were replaced by an Americanized version.

Military personnel at other American military bases in Mexico, Australia and underwater in the Pacific do not use an extraterrestrial lexicon.

The original language of the Anunnaki is still intact and is currently being used by top American scientists and researchers who work in secret American-Aliens military bases in the United States and Mexico.

In 1947, the first attempt was made by American linguists, who previously worked at the OSS (Precursor to the CIA), to decipher it. They tried to compare it with the Sumerian, Hebrew, Armenian and Phoenician Alphabet, languages which are directly derived from the Anunnaki's written language. The problem they faced and could not resolve were the geometrical symbols included in the written Anunnaki's texts. But in 1956, they cracked down the puzzle.

Those mathematical figures hold great secrets regarding an alien advanced technology used for peaceful and constructive purposes.

The American military intelligence and what's left from Dr. Fermi's group at Los Alamos wanted to use this alien technology for military purposes.

The Anunnaki have two kinds or styles of languages; one is spoken and the other one is written. The spoken language is the easiest one to learn, and it is used by the Anunnaki's population.

The written one is exclusively used in books and consists of twenty-six letters. Seven of these letters represent the planets that surround their planet.

*** *** ***

24-What Is The Anunnaki Liquid Light?

The Answer

What Is The Anunnaki Liquid Light?

- The Liquid-Light is an Anunnaki electro-plasma substance that appears like luminous watery substance, and it is called "Nou-Rah Shams."
- In Anakh (Anunnaki language), Menou-Ra actually means the following: Nou, or Nour, or sometimes Menour, representing light.

It has the same meaning in many Semitic languages. Shams means sun. The Ulema in Egypt, Syria, Iraq and Lebanon use the same word in their opening ceremony.

- Sometimes, the word Nour becomes Nar, which means fire.

This is intentional, because the Ulema, like the Phoenicians, believed in fire as a symbolic procedure to purify the thoughts. This created the word Min-Nawar, meaning the enlightened or surrounded with light.

- If you know any Hebrew, you might remember that Menorah means a lamp. It's all connected. Later, the Illuminati used it as well.

*** *** ***

25-What Is Mah-RIT? Is It Anunnaki Steroids?

The Answer

What Is Mahrit? Is It Anunnaki Steroids?

- Mah-RIT is humanity's early form/formula of what we call today steroids; an early genetic product created by the Anunnaki in the ancient Phoenician city of Amrit, in Syria co-built by the remnants of the Anunnaki and early Phoenicians from Tyre and Sidon.

Amrit is one of the most puzzling, mysterious and enigmatic cities in recorded history. It was the stage for a cosmic war between many ancient nations; the birth of the "Olympiads"; and the world's first Anunnaki-Phoenician medical center.
But recent archeological excavations on the Island of Arwad revealed that this island gave birth to the "Olympiads", and not Amrit as it was suggested by historians.

- Mah-RIT was first used by Inanna when she created the first 7 prototypes of the human race.
- Phoenicians used Mah-Rit quite often. It was supplied by the priests of god Melkart.

*** *** ***

157

26-What Is The Anunnaki ME.nou-Ra?

The Answer

What Is The Anunnaki ME.nou-Ra?

- MEnour "ME.nou-Ra" is a sort of a light (Plasma laser) used by the Anunnaki to purify the body and thoughts.
- All Anunnaki students entering the classroom in an Anunnaki Academy must purify their bodies and minds.
- The purification exercise occurs inside a small room, entirely made of shimmering white marble.
- In the middle of the room, there is a basin, made of the same material, and filled with a substance called Nou-Rah Shams; an electro-plasma substance that appears like 'liquid-light.'
- It actually means, in Anakh, The Liquid of Light.
- Nou, or Nour, or sometimes Menour, or Menou-Ra, means light.
- Shams means sun.
- Nour in Arabic means light.
- The Ulema in Egypt, Syria, Iraq and Lebanon use the same word in their opening ceremony.
- Sometimes, the word Nour becomes Nar, which means fire.
- This is intentional, because the Ulemas, like the Phoenicians, believed in fire as a symbolic procedure to purify the thoughts.

27-Anunnaki Code Predictions And Revelations

The Answer

Code Predictions and Revelations

What is the Anunnaki Code?

The Anunnaki Code is an effective tool to foresee forthcoming events in the immediate and long term future.

The expression or term "foreseeing" is never used in the Anakh language and by extraterrestrials because they don't foresee and predict.

They just calculate and formulate. In spatial terms, they don't even measure things and distances, because time and space do not exist as two separate "presences" in their dimensions.

However, on Nibiru, Anunnaki are fully aware of all these variations, and the human concept of time and space, and have the capability of separating time and space, and/or combining them into one single dimension, or one single "frame of existence".

Anunnaki understand "time" differently from us. For instance, on Nibiru, there are no clocks and no watches. They are useless.

Then you might ask: "So, how do they measure time? How do they know what time is it... now or after 10 minutes, or in one hour from now?"

The answer is simple: If you don't need time, you don't need to measure it.

However, on Nibiru, Anunnaki experience time and space as we do on earth. And they do measure objects, substances, distances and locations as we do on earth. But they rarely do.

The Anunnaki (in addition to the Nordics and Lyrans) are the only known extraterrestrials in the universe to look like humans, and in many instances, they share several similarities with the human race. This physiognomic resemblance explains to a certain degree, the reason for Anunnaki to use "time".

To "calculate and formulate" information and to acquire data, Anunnaki consult the "Code Screen". Consulting the screen means: Reading "Events Sequences". Every single event in the cosmos in any dimension has a code; call it for now a "number".

Nothing happens in the universe without a reason. The universe has its own logic that the human mind cannot understand. In many instances, the "logic of Numbers" dictates and creates events. And not all created events are understood by the extraterrestrials. This is why they resort to the "Code Screen".

Activation of the "Code Screen"

Activating the Code requires two actions or procedures:

1-Preparing the grid or cadre.

This demands clearing all the previous data stored in the "pockets" of the net.

"Net" resembles space net as usually used by quantum physics scientists. They do in fact compare space to a net. According to their theories, the "net" as the landscape of time and space bends under the weight of a "ball" rotating at a maximum speed.

The centrifugal effect produced by the ball alters the shape of the net, and consequently the fabric of space. And by altering space, time changes automatically.

And as time changes, speed and distances change simultaneously.

Same principle applies to stretching and cleaning up the net of the screen containing a multitude of codes of the Anunnaki.

"Pockets" means the exact dimension and a space an object occupies on the universe net or landscape. No more than one object or one substance occupies one single pocket; this is by earth standard and human level of knowledge.

In other parallel words, more than one object or one substance can be infused in one single pocket. But this could lead to loss of memory.

Yes, objects and substances have memory too, just like human beings; some are called:

- a-"space memory",
- b-"time memory",
- c-"string memory",
- d-"astral memory",
- e-"metal memory", etc…the list is endless.

Thus, all pockets containing previous data are cleared. And now they are ready to absorb and store new data. How do they clear the data? I have no clues. And no human on the face of the earth knows!

2-Feeding the "Pockets": Retrieving Data.

All sorts and sizes of data are retrieved and stored through the "Conduit".

The "Conduit" is an electroplasmic substance implanted into the cells of the brain. I am not going to repeat the lengthy description of the characteristics and properties of the "Conduit". Please refer to my book "Anunnaki Encyclopedia".

3-Viewing the Data:

Retrieved data and information are viewed through the "Miraya", also called "Cosmic Mirror". Some refer to it as "Akashic Records". It is not! In-depth description of the "Miraya" is provided in the book "Anunnaki Encyclopedia"

4-Revisiting The Past:

Can the Anunnaki revisit the past? In other words, can they travel back in time? The answer is yes. This concept might seem absurd to many. But quantum physics professors and theorists have already explained this in papers they have published. And once again, let me remind you that I have explained the phenomenon of going back in time in the "Anunnaki Encyclopedia."

5-Going Forward in the Future

Can the Anunnaki go forward in time and meet with the future? Yes, they can! An Ulema told me that future events have already happened at some level and in some spheres. It is just a matter of a "waiting period" for the mind to see it.

6-Did the Anunnaki Predict Anything?

Yes, they did. But please remember, the Anunnaki do not "predict".

They just "see" the future as briefly explained before. The book "Anunnaki Encyclopedia" listed some of their predictions. Here are some excerpts from the book:

2,034 A.D.: The secret code of the Bible will be revealed. Part of the code will be used to predict the future. Humanity will finally know the true identity of Yeshua (Jesus), Moshe (Moses) and Mouhammad (Mohammad). The original voice of Jesus in Aramaic, several Biblical figures and greatest personages in our history will be found and recorded on the "Memory Screen" replacing tapes and CDs.

2,031-2,033 A.D.: Humans will have spatial-galactic-extra-sensorial faculties' implants. And Electro-magnetic telepathy will be developed, thus reducing time and space limitations. Many will be able to revisit the past and foresee the immediate future.

2,029 A.D.: Several American bases will be created on Mars and the moon. The Americans will reverse the anti-gravity laws. Several stargates will fill our skies, and become fully operational and totally controlled by American scientists.
Humans will be able to store their memory on a computer chip. Cinema will become 3 dimensionally animated.
American, Russian and French astrophysicists and scientists will discover and recapture voices and sounds from humanity's past, going back to the dawn of creation.

2,028 A.D.: The Vatican becomes an icon of the past. Life expectancy in the United States (lifespan average) will become 130 years. Americans will conquer many diseases, to name a few: AIDS, cancer, Alzheimer,

169

thanks to new technology and very advanced scientific knowledge gained from extraterrestrials.
Official extraterrestrial embassies and delegations will be established on earth.

2,027-2,026 A.D.: By November 2,026, The United States will resurface as a major key player in world's affairs and regain its universal leadership. The American Dollar will have a face-lift.
Puerto Rico becomes a major spatial base for extraterrestrials. Many extraterrestrial bases will be created on earth, the majority in the United States.
By the end of 2,027, the United States will emerge as the absolute and ultimate power on earth, and will intensify its cooperation with several extraterrestrial civilizations. This will lead to the creation of a new extraterrestrial-terrestrial lexicon on earth.

2,026 A.D.: A new powerful and global religion will be established on earth, created by new scientific development and a direct contact with extraterrestrial civilizations. Many will convert to this new religion except the Muslims. Islam and a form of extraterrestrial-spiritual religion will become the two major religions on earth.
Islamabad will be declared the official capital of Islam on earth. The United Arab Emirates, Qatar, Kuwait, Bahrain, and Saudi Arabia will fall in the hands of the World Islamic Council controlled by Pakistan. India will lose Kashmere.

2,025 A.D.: Afro-Americans become the majority in the United States. Islam will unify all Muslim countries, and several Islamic countries will acquire the atomic bomb. Muslims in Europe will constitute 72% of the French population, 64% of the Scandinavian countries, and 91% of the African Continent.

A major military confrontation between Muslim countries and Israel will decimate many nations on the globe. Tibet will become an independent country.

A military alliance between Pakistan, Malaysia, Indonesia and 29 Muslim countries will shift the world's military, nuclear, commerce and peace balance. England will be totally alienated in Europe.

However by the end of 2,025 England will regain global influence. Lebanon will be fully absorbed by Islam, and a major Christian Lebanese exodus will begin; many will settle in Canada, Brazil and France. Malta will play a major role on the map of world's affairs. The Anunnaki will interfere to put an end to the humans' madness.

2,022 A.D.: Threat to humanity:

2,022 A.D., September. The Higher Council of the Anunnaki learned that the aliens intend to attack earth on a massive scale by 2,022. A major confrontation with aliens will happen in September 2,022; the consequences are not totally clear, nor predictable.

However, extraordinary events will occur, including global ecological changes, extraordinary advance in medicine, a global unified monetary system that will unite the market of 125 countries, but the United States will refuse to take part in it, and this refusal could lead to the collapse of the American financial influence worldwide, and force American banks' branches abroad to go out of business. The American Dollar is no longer a hard currency.

But the United States will remain a super power with global influence.

*** *** ***

28-What Is The Secret Meaning Of Haf-nah, The Symbol Of Mushrooms?

The Answer

What Is The Secret Meaning Of Haf-nah, The Symbol Of Mushrooms?

Mushroom was a very important symbol in the early Ana'kh

Although it might appear insignificant and silly in the context of extraterrestrial civilizations and Anunnaki's literature, the mushroom was a very important symbol in the early Anakh (Anunnaki language) scripts given to the Phoenicians and later on to King Solomon. Mushroom in Anak is "Haf-nah", and it represents many things such as:
1-fecundity,
2-occult
3-power;
4-heredity;
5-life;
6-genetical reproduction;
7-and even a sexual symbol referring to a woman.

Ancient Sumerian, Persians and Phoenicians myths tell us how patriarchs used an extraction from mushroom and mixed it with an Anunnaki female DNA to create a secret race of creatures capable of building huge edifices and temples.

Legend has it that the Templars learned this secret while digging in the basements and underground tunnels of the temple of King Solomon.

The Book of Rama-Dosh elaborated on this mixture and described how "Haf-nah" was used to create an extraordinary quasi-human race capable of performing miracles and teleporting stones of an immense dimension.

In the early Phoenician language, "Haf-na" meant:

- a-hand;
- b-grabbing;
- c-instrument.

Ironically and interestingly enough, if you read the Christian Arabic translation of the Bible you will find this phrase: "Haf-nat Tourab". And this is mind-boggling, because it refers to the creation of Adam, in other words the creation of the human race.

In Arabic, "Haf-na" means:

- a-What a hand can grab;
- b-A small quantity.

The contemporary meaning of the word "Tourab" in Arabic is:

- a-sand;
- b-dirt.

Now, if you add Haf-na+Tourab, you get this: The hand grabs dirt. And this is how the Christian Arabic Bible interprets the creation of Adam; God grabbed with his hand dirt from the ground.

So, the mushroom, hand, and dirt are enigmatically connected in the creation's script of the ancients.

The Mushroom, Anunnaki and Knights Templar.

The meaning of the name of the great Perseus, founder of the Perseid Dynasty, and builder of the Citadel of

176

Mycenae is: "The Place of the Mushroom", and various illustrations of the mushroom appear abundantly on churches' columns.

Another striking example is the figure of the Biblical Melchizedek that appeared on a façade of the "Cathedral de Chartre" in France, holding a chalice in the shape of a mushroom, symbolizing life, and perhaps the "Holy Grail", as interpreted in the literature of Cathars, Templars, and many enlightened eastern secret societies. It was also interpreted as the "Divine-Human Vessel", meaning the womb of Virgin Mary; the very womb that gave birth to Jesus.

In ancient Phoenician and Akkadian traditions closely related to the Anunnaki, the mushroom as a chalice represents the creative power of the female. More precisely, the fecundity of a female Anunnaki goddess, giver of life and all living creatures.
This fecundity source came in the form of a mitochondrial DNA.
Also, the secret extracted liquid of the mushroom represented the "Light Liquid" known also as "Elixir of Life".

On many Templars' pillars and Bourj (upper part of a medieval fortress or a castle) in Syria, Malta and Lebanon, the mushroom is carefully illustrated as a "Flower of Life" known to the Phoenicians, Habiru (Hebrew), early Arabs, Sumerians and Anunnaki as:
- a-Wardah;
- b-Ward;
- c-Vardeh (Almost the same word in all these languages), symbolizing the "blooming of life".

177

At one point in history, the mushroom's figure was used by the Templars of St. John of Malta as the symbol of the Holy Grail.

And in other passages, the mushroom represented a head; the head of a leader. Some historians thought that the leader was Baphomet, while others believed that is was "Noah", and another group believed it was the Prophet Mohammed, and finally, there is a group of learned masters who claimed that is was the "Khalek of Markabah".

Familiar?

Khalek is "God", and "Markabah" is a spaceship (UFO).

The Anunnaki's mushroom symbol gave birth to the "Cult of Head". There is nothing in the world more stimulating and captivating than deciphering buried ancient linguistic-religious symbols and languages.

*** *** ***

29-Who Is Nafar JinMarkah? Was He The Early Human On Three Legs?

The Answer

Who Is Nafar JinMarkah? Was He The Early Human On Three Legs?

- Nafar Jinmarkah, is the name of humans on three legs: The Anunnaki were geneticists and engineers with a strong appreciation for aesthetics.

Per contra, the Igigi created a very primitive form of living beings on earth, exactly as humans created unappealing early forms and shapes of robots, and related mechanical devices, at the dawn of robotics. These robots were functional but not pretty to look at, and the Igigi considered the early quasi-humans to be not much more than machines with limited mental faculties.

- The early forms of humans were created by the Igigi, and looked like apes.
- The earth was extremely cold at that time, and the Igigi had to cover the human bodies with lots of hair to protect them from the elements. It took the quasi-human race thousands of years to evolve into an early human form, and even then not totally human, still looking like apes.
- Some of them had bizarre skulls and facial bones.
- The Igigi actually experimented a bit with the early human-forms.
- First, they created the "Nafar Jinmarkah" meaning 'individual on three legs.'

- They consisted of a very strong physical body but lacked agility. Those bodies were created to carry heavy weight. The three legs' purpose was to support heavy loads they could lift and carry.
- Later on, the Igigi worked on a new human form that consisted of a body with two legs, to bring speed and better agility.
- Yet, early humans remained terrifying, nothing like the Biblical descriptions.
- The Igigi tried four times. They experimented in four different ways. Each time, they faced a problem in designing the human skull. Early Igigi creators did not want to put brains in the skull so human-forms-bodies would not think. These early human-forms were the world's first robots.
- The Anunnaki were the ones who created the brains for the humans.
- These early brains contained two million cells. But the Anunnaki too worked several times on the prototypes of humans. In their final genetic experiments, the Anunnaki programmed humans with the thirteen original faculties.

*** *** ***

30-Do Anunnaki Have Extra-Senses And Particular Powers?

The Answer

Do Anunnaki Have Extra-Senses And Particular Powers?

- The Anunnaki have an astonishing range of extra-senses and incomprehensible powers.
- Almost all extraterrestrials possess multiple physical-mental faculties that can be called extra-senses.
- The Anunnaki and the Artyrians have 13 different kinds of extra-senses, ranging from physio-biological to mental-sensorial. They are NOT neurological.
- The Naryans have 17 senses. Some of the most fascinating senses are:
- **a-**The ability of freeing themselves from the limitation of time and space and sensing the "ultra dimension"; in other words, they are able to feel and sense the infinitesimal frequencies that constitute the dividing waves or walls between each dimension and/or multiple universes.
- Those dividing lines are waves and they expand and react spatially like rubber bands. There are no other words or expressions in the human vocabularies we can use to describe these "existences".
- **b-**They can totally eliminate and sense the effect of heat and cold and mentally regulate the temperature degrees of the environment. Also they can adjust others' bodies' temperature for health and therapeutic reasons, because they can

185

sense the body's weaknesses and strengths. In terrestrial terms, they can see the aura. But it goes beyond aura, because aura is produced bio-organically and can be detected either visually or through scientific apparatus.

- The Anunnaki can easily jam any communication and transmission device on earth, and disable any military and scientific apparatus and equipment instantaneously.
- Extraterrestrials and particularly the Anunnaki and the Grays know very well all missiles installations and locations on earth, whether on the surface, underwater or underground. They can disable their delivery systems in a fraction of a second.
- The Anunnaki have conquered the laws of anti-gravity.
- The Anunnaki can bend time and space.
- The Anunnaki can navigate the universe and reach unimaginable destinations and travel mind boggling distances in a very short time using "Babs", stargates and wormholes.
- An Anunnaki can transpose and transport himself/herself to several places simultaneously, and appear in the same time in multiple locations, always conserving his/her properties and physical-mental capacities.
- This can be done through various techniques such as using a "Double", another "Copy" of himself/herself, de-fragmenting the molecules of his/her physical body and recreating identical molecules in another dimension. Anunnaki are physical, mental, vibrational and multi-dimensional.

- Anunnaki can transmute metals into any other metal, including gold.
- Anunnaki can alter the properties of any liquid, soft and hard substances.
- Anunnaki can live up to 400,000 years.
- Through their "Miraya" (Cosmic Monitor), the Anunnaki can watch and follow any event happening on many other planets.
- Anunnaki can travel into the future and the past. They can alter the events they have created in the past, and influence occurrences to happen in the future.

***   ***   ***

31-Are There Animals
On Nibiru?

The Answer

Are There Animals On Nibiru?

Answer: YES! And they are well-treated!

- The Anunnaki believe that the early animals on earth were created by evil spirits (Mental- non dimensional entities.) Anunnaki did not want to create animals.
- While working in their genetic laboratories on creating new life forms, outside the human or quasi human border line, and by trial and error, one formula produced cats.
- The cat in the Anunnaki's language is called Bessa.
- In Coptic and Arabic and other Semitic language, the cat is called Bess or Bessa; strange similarity for two separate civilizations that are apart by million light years.
- The Anunnaki, upon noticing that the female cats responded joyfully to the sound of music and water falls, they added to their genetic formula an extra sensorial faculty to enhance their hearing.
- There is something unusual in the Anunnaki's genetic creation of cats, because their cats don't have gender.
- Only female cats live on their planet, and they reproduce constantly without mating obviously;

their reproduction process occurs in genetic laboratories.

- One of the gifts that the Anunnaki gave the early friendly monarchs of the earth was a set of cats. You can see this gift illustrated in the history and mythology of Egypt.
- This is another connection or relation between the lineage of the early pharaohs and the Anunnaki.
- Also the cats of the Anunnaki have psychic powers.
- Although they don't sense fear and danger like earth's cats, they predict weather and atmospheric anomalies.
- And another unique characteristic – they can talk.
- They talk to the Anunnaki via vocal expressions. It's not a fully cohesive language that uses nouns, adjectives, verbs, or sentences; it is a series of uttered words and conversational expressions.
- Only one kind of cat exists. And this breed looks a bit like Siamese but with white fur and rainbow of blue and gray around the neck. They are double the size of our cats. The color of their eyes is very light blue.
- Birds: There is infinity of types and colors. All genetically created by the Anunnaki, and they all sing. And yes, they give eggs.
- On Ashtari (Nibiru) and Zeta Reticuli, you will not find insects, only butterflies, because they blend well with the beauty of the landscape and they were also created by genetic formulas. Interestingly enough, the genetic formulas were

not created by highly advanced scientists, as on earth.

- The Anunnaki's children created those life forms, and genetic engineering is part of their schools' curricula.

*** *** ***

32-What Kind Of Relation Eve And Her Children Had With God And The Anunnaki?

The Answer

What Kind Of Relation Eve And Her Children Had With God And The Anunnaki?

There is a vast literature about Eve, and lots of contradictory accounts about her true nature, her origin, her DNA, and above all, her relation with the Anunnaki, the "Gods" and the Judeo-Christian-Muslim God. Eve appeared in the Sumerian texts, in Phoenicians epics, in the Bible, in the Quran, in the Gnostics books, and in the Ulema's manuscripts. Eve story in the Bible is the less credible one.

According to the Gnostic Books, Eve had a direct relationship with a God called the Ruler. The nature and identity of the rulers are not clear. But an alert mind can assume that the ruler was the God of the earth, the creator of the human race.

- The Sumerian texts convey almost a similar message. In many passages of the Anunnaki-Sumerian scriptures, the Anunnaki Creators of the human race were physically intimate with their creations.
- Enki was the most visible one. In the Gnostics books, the "Ruler" is a divinity and a creator. In The Sumerian texts, EN.Ki is a king, a god and a creator.

- Both created the same woman. However, according to the Sumerian texts and Anunnaki Mythology, it is not absolutely clear whether EN.KI was the original and sole creator of Eve, because numerous Akkadian/Sumerian deities participated in the creation of mankind, such as Angel Gabriel known as Gb'r, Inanna, to name a few.

Quite often, humans who were genetically created by the Anunnaki were "produced" from and by a mixture of the DNA of an Anunnaki, usually a god or a goddess, and an earthy element.

This element was described as either clay or specie of a primitive human being. The intervention of an Anunnaki god was a prerequisite.

Thousands of years later, the Bible told us that Eve too received a divine help in the creation of her first two sons; they were fathered by the "Lord" not by Adam.

This could and would astonish the Christians. Eve conceived Cain and Abel with the help of God. Only her third son Seth was the result of her union with Adam. And Seth came to life in Adam's likeness. So how did Cain and Abel look like?

The Bible does not provide an answer. From Genesis: 4:1 "...and she bore Cain saying."I have gotten a man with the help of the Lord. And again, she bore his brother Abel..." Genesis 5: 3 "When Adam had lived a hundred and thirty years, he became the father of a son in his own likeness, after his image, and named him Seth."

The Gnostics books shed a bright light on this situation; Cain was created by the Anunnaki god EN.KI and a woman called KaVa, (Also Havvah and Hawwa) which is the original name of Eve in the ancient texts written thousands of years before the Bible was written and

198

assembled. This is the official version of the Gnostics. This means that Cain is not 100% human. Cain's blood is ¾ or ½ Anunnaki. The other two sons of Eve, Abel called "Hevel", and Seth called "Sata-Na-il" were less than ½ genetically Anunnaki, because they were the offspring of KaVa (Eve) and Ata.Bba (Original name of Adam).

- Cain was superior to his brother Abel at so many levels, because he was the offspring of an Anunnaki.
- Abel was inferior to Cain, because he was the offspring of an earthy element. The superiority of Cain was documented in the Bible, because the Bible (Old and New Testaments) clearly stated that Cain "rose far above Abel"!

What can we conclude from this hypothesis?
We can conclude that
1-Eve and Adam were not from the same race. Genetically, they were different.
2-Consequently, the offspring people (first human race) of Eve were the result of a breeding by Gods.
3-The children of Abel and Cain were genetically modified to fit the scenario of the Anunnaki.
4-The creation of the human race happened earlier, much earlier than the date suggested by Jewish, Christian and Muslim scriptures.
5-All human races came from the primordial female element: EVE.

*** *** ***

33-What Is The Nature Of The Ulema?

The Answer

What are the Ulema? Are they gods, angels, and spirits?

*** *** ***

Note: The Ulema are not the Anunnaki-Ulema.

The Ulema are not gods, angels or spirits.
The Ulema are divided into two categories, called "Dara-Ja".
1-Category One: "The Enlightened Teachers". They are humans living on earth. And they are called "Mou.NA Wa.Rin"
2-Category Two: The super beings, called "Guardians". They live in various higher physical and non-physical dimensions.

1-Category One:
The Enlightened Teachers "Mou.NA Wa.Rin"

They are a group of thinkers, philosophers and scientists. They are the custodians of important books and ancient manuscripts about the origin of mankind, the creation of the universe and human races, and a multitude of subjects pertaining to vital aspects of humanity, "intelligent beings" and other dimensions that are closely connected to humans.
The Ulema group was also called the "Society of the Book of Rama-Dosh".
The Ulema do not discuss religions. Although, many of them belong to various religious beliefs and faiths. Three

203

of the most important manuscripts (very ancient texts) they keep in utmost secrecy and with an enormous reverence are:

1-**The Book of Rama-Dosh,** also called the Book of Radosh.

Main topic: The origin of mankind, and how various extraterrestrial races genetically created the human race.

2-**Shams El Maaref Al Koubra** (The Sun of the Great Knowledge).

Main topic: The study of superior beings who live in higher physical and non physical dimensions, and who are watching over us.

3-**Al Hak** (Justice and Truth).

Main topic: Laws that allow mankind to live righteously on earth and allow human beings to prepare themselves for the next life. Guidance for the next journey is provided in metaphors and parables.

The Ulema group was created during the time of Hiram, the Phoenician King of Tyre. It included illustrious astronomers, astrologers, physicians, mathematicians, scientists, philosophers and metaphysicists from Sumer, Phoenicia, Syria, Palestine, Egypt and Greece. Later on, leading figures of the Knights of St John of Malta, The Templars, The Wise Men of Arwad, and Hiram-Grand Orient Masonic Rites' members joined the Ulema group. Mou.NA Wa.Rin means: Those who have received the light of the great knowledge.

2-Category Two:
The super beings, called "Guardians"

The "Guardians" are not human beings. And they are not spirits either.

Humans were taught to believe that the world (seen and unseen) consists of a physical life on earth, and a spiritual life after death.

The Ulema's views are different.

According to The Book of Sun of the Great Knowledge, the world or universe usually referred to as *existence* "Wu-Jud" contains more than a physical life and a spiritual life.

Wu Jud consists of 11 dimensions. Humans are aware of three dimensions on earth. The fourth is the one that exists in the next life.

That is the limit of their understanding and interpretation of the world; the physical and spiritual.

To the Ulema, existence, including human existence goes beyond the fourth dimension. The "Guardians" live in the fourth, fifth, six, and seventh dimensions. In the eight dimension, live the "Ultimate Ones". And so on...

Thus, the "Guardians" who live in the fourth, fifth, six and seventh dimensions are noble entities who regularly communicate with chosen human beings and enlightened teachers for various reasons and purposes.

The "Guardians" are not physical beings, however, they can manifest to us in any shape or form using a "Plasmic" organism or substance that the human mind cannot comprehend. The Ulema receive knowledge and guidance from the "Guardians".

What is the relationship between humans and Ulema?

1-The Physical Ulema:

The "physical" Ulema who live on earth are not very much different from the rest of us, as physical humans.

But on other levels, they are very different from human beings. For instance (to name a few)

1-They do not age as rapidly as we do. A seventy year old Ulema look like a forty five year old man.

2-Ulema live longer than ordinary human beings. Their lifespan on earth is approximately 135 years.

3-They are vegetarians. Yes, they do drink, but with moderation. Some smoke, but not cigarettes.
Their pipe tobacco is made out of aromatic dried fruits.

4-They have an enormous compassion toward animals. In fact, they communicate so well with animals, the majority of them except crocodiles, snakes, insects carrying bacteria and diseases, and four reptiles' species. Animals sense their presence and welcome them. Ulema have developed a sign language to facilitate their communication with animals. And usually, animals respond in the same manner.

5-Ulema are well-versed in many languages. And they are fond of languages of ancient civilizations, including those of vanished cultures.
Ulema learn foreign languages very easily and rapidly. Usually, an Ulema learns a foreign language in less than a week.

6-Ulema can read a voluminous book and memorize it in its entirety in less than three hours.

7-Ulema can foresee the future and predict events to happen in several dimensions, including our own.

8-Ulema are in constant contact with the "Guardians".

9-Ulema knowledge in arts, science, history and religions is limitless. Etc…

These qualities and gifts allow them to fully understand the human psyche, read our minds, and sympathize with our tastes, needs and aspirations. They are socially active, however, they do not reveal themselves to the rest of us, nor get involved in groups' activities.

They dislike organized religions, politics, fanaticism, prejudices, stock markets, financial interests, publicity, egoism, and excessive authority.

It is not so easy to gain membership in their groups and societies. Membership is by invitation only. And the membership procedures and initiation process, formalities, and rituals are rigorous. Many applicants have failed because of the tests they had to go through.

2-The Non-Physical Ulema:

The non-physical Ulema do not reveal themselves to us. They communicate with the physical Ulema on an exclusive basis through:

- 1-Secret codes and a visual language.
- 2-Ectoplasmic apparitions.
- 3-Transmission of mind.
- 4-Visitations through "Ba'abs".
- 5-Telepathy triggered by a "Conduit" implanted and activated in the brain' cells.

Ordinary human beings are not trained nor prepared to communicate with them. They can't see them, and they can't sense their presence, even though sometimes they are very close to them.

*** *** ***

34-What Are The Plans Of The Anunnaki For Their Return In 2022?

The Answer

What are the plans of the Anunnaki for their return in 2022?

The Anunnaki are coming back to clean the earth.

As was mentioned in a previous question, they created the earth, started developing the life forms, fostered the evolutionary process, and managed to accumulate an enormous amount of useful knowledge, all of which they telepathically transferred to Nibiru, where it was much appreciated.

Unfortunately, the knowledge leaked to the Grays at Zeta Reticuli, and they decided to use the humans, and sometimes the cattle, in their doomed experiments that were geared to save their own miserable race.

While doing this, they sadly contaminated the pure genetic material the Anunnaki so painstakingly created, and the humans that resulted were no longer suitable for the study.

That was the reason why the Anunnaki deserted their research on earth.

Now, after receiving pertinent information over the last forty years, the Anunnaki had decided to come back and clean up their creations.

Whether they are doing it out of benevolence, or because they wish to pursue their laboratory work, we do not as yet know.

But one thing is clear – any human being heavily tainted by the Grays' DNA will be destroyed.

Some, who are lightly contaminated, will be evaluated further, but in another dimension, so as not to endanger the cleaned up earth.

Those who are not contaminated will remain on earth, which will be immeasurably improved by the removal of the contaminated humans.

The Anunnaki know who is contaminated, and what is the contamination level, by using the Conduit, so to them it is extremely easy to make the selection. This process of selection will be extremely fast, a matter of minutes.

Since most humans do not have a functional Conduit, only a latent one, we must use other ways to find out what is our chances for survival so we can take steps to improve the odds; this will be done individually, each person must examine his or her level.

You will not be helped by joining a religious group, or going to therapy, or any other form of relying on someone else. You will have to do your own work, but it is not difficult to find out.

Figuring it out requires thought and introspection only.

The Grays' DNA

The Grays' DNA have created greed, violence, and unbelievable cruelty within our nature.

Such characteristics were not part of the original DNA material used to create humans, since the original DNA was given by the Anunnaki themselves, who had intended to create humans in their image.

Therefore, each person must examine his or her life carefully. The list of offences is extremely long, but here are some examples of people who are contaminated by the Grays' DNA.

They are divided into three groups.

If any of these traits exist in you, if you have committed any of these atrocities, try to remove them as soon as possible from your life – if you wish to survive after 2022. But even with all your hard work, there is no guarantee.

People who exhibit heavy Grays' DNA contamination

- Those who torture or support torture by others, for any purpose whatsoever
- Murderers (unless in self defense, which sometimes occurs in situations such as domestic abuse by a contaminated spouse)
- Rapists
- Child molesters
- Child abusers
- Senior abusers
- Spouse abusers
- Those who commit violent robberies
- Illicit drug manufacturers, distributors and pushers
- Those who engage in enslaving women, girls and young boys in prostitution rings
- Criminals who use their form of religion as an excuse for their heinous crimes; this include all religious fanatics, such as suicide bombers
- Those who destroy lives by depriving them of ways to support themselves, for their own greed. This include the top echelon of corporate executives, who have lost any sense of humanity in their treatment of thousands of people and feel that this is "strictly business"
- Elected officials who have sold out for power and greed, and who are willing to destroy their own countries to aggrandize themselves

- Elected officials who are willingly participating in destroying the ecology of the planet because of their close association with the oil and other forms of commercial energies producing countries and their corrupt rulers.
- Any politician, military personnel, or anyone else who is engaging in trade with the Grays, allowing them to continue the atrocities in exchange for technical and military knowledge
- Lawyers and judges who play games at the legal system for their own gain, sending free, child molesters, murderers, and other violent offenders in the name of "reasonable doubt"
- Those who destroy lives and reputations by "identity theft"
- Those who torment animals.
- These include not only people who hurt and mutilate animals for their own sick pleasure, but also those who support dog fights, cockfights and bullfights, those who beat their horses, donkeys, or dogs, those who "legally" mutilate cats by removing their claws or hurting their vocal cords, owners of puppy mills who force female dogs to reproduce by "animal rape," and those who abandon their animals, or chain them indefinitely, sometimes allowing them to die by such neglect.

People who exhibit medium Grays' DNA contamination:

- People who believe that discipline requires physical punishment (in children or adults)

214

- Middle echelon executives who "only take orders" from their superiors as their corporations are destroying the economy of their own countries to save their own skin
- Those, who in the name of fashion and beauty, have hurt countless young girls who have succumbed to eating disorders, some of whom have actually died, while the owners and designers made a fortune for themselves
- Irresponsible parents who allow their children to grow up with Grays' values rather than human and Anunnaki values
- Hunters of animals who believe they are doing it only for food but do not feel a joy in killing
- Owners of "factory farms" whose animals are not tormented, but live a miserable life
- People who eat any form of meat (the Anunnaki believe in strict vegetarian diet, supplemented by milk and eggs from animals that are treated humanely and allowed to live out their life comfortably and die naturally)

People who exhibit light Grays' DNA contamination

- People who are willing to advertise products that may be harmful, for gain
- People who are willing to import products that may be harmful, for gain
- People who object to social reform that may help the greater number of others, such as health care or better equalization of income, for gain
- People who are engaged in the fur trade

- People who are willing to influence others through brain wash advertising, such as the cosmetic industry, for gain
- Racists, sexists, and ageists, who are willing to allow their prejudices to influence their behaviour to others
- People who are willing to spend millions of dollars on frivolous pursuits (diamond studded collars for dogs, who really don't care about anything but love and food? $200,000 wedding cakes?) while millions around them are starving
- People actively engaged in aggressive take-overs, thus destroying the livelihood of many
- Anyone deliberately sending a computer virus for "fun"

This is only a partial listing. Examine your heart, there may be other reasons to assume you are contaminated. There are only 12 years to the final date.

*** *** ***

35-What Will Happen In 2022, When The Anunnaki Return?

The Answer

What Will Happen In 2022, When The Anunnaki Return?

Many things at so many levels: Physical, spiritual, mental, multidimensional, vibrational, intellectual, and religious.

As mentioned in a previous question, the Anunnaki are returning in 2022 to clean the earth. This will happen through a cataclysmic event, the like of which can hardly even be imagined by us, but is child play to the Anunnaki, who have done it all before on other planets, many times. The procedure will take a very short time, a few minutes only, but is, as always, elaborately and securely planned by the Anunnaki.

The Anunnaki will bring a bubble of a special substance, resembling anti-matter but not destructive, and cause it to touch the earth's atmosphere. It will be exactly the size of earth.

As soon as the two globes touch, all the humans that have been lucky enough not to be contaminated by Grays' DNA, and all the animals, plants, and those inanimate material which the Anunnaki wish to preserve (such as beautiful and historic monuments, art-filled museums, and great libraries, in addition to the homes of those saved) will be stripped from earth and absorbed into the bubble.

The fish, and other animals who need water, will be taken to a created ocean within the bubble. The birds will have plenty of places to perch on. Nothing will be hurt or damaged – the humans and animals will feel nothing – they will be secure within the bubble. It is unlikely that they will even retain a clear memory of the event, because the Anunnaki would not wish them to be traumatized.

Then, the earth will be cleaned of all our pollution. For lack of better description, try to imagine a huge vacuum cleaner removing all the landfills, eliminating all the plastics, all the dirt, all the smog from the air, and all the filth from the ocean. In a few short minutes, the earth will be sparkling clean, a pristine planet, the way it was when the Anunnaki had first created it. How they dispose of the garbage is not clear to us – it involves a very high technology which we simply do not as yet understand.

The beautiful clean planet is now ready to be repopulated, and in an instant, the humans, animals, plants, and inanimate objects would be returned to earth. Anunnaki guides will be there for the humans, who would naturally need quite a bit of help to adjust to the new life.

In the meantime, the issue of the rest of humanity is resolved as well. As mentioned in a previous question, there are three groups of humans the Anunnaki will attend to. Those who are not contaminated have already been taken back to the cleaned planet.

Those who are heavily contaminated, and who are engaging in cruelty, greed, and violence for their own gain, have no chance at all.

They will simply be destroyed, and there is no need to even think about them any further.

What is left are those who are the medium-level of contamination, and the lighter level.

These groups had received a warning to mend their lives, fourteen years before the event of 2022. Some of the people of light level contamination would have completely cleaned themselves through their efforts, and therefore would have been transferred, as clean beings, into the bubble.

Others had remained lightly contaminated.

Those of medium level contamination, who obviously require more work, would be divided into those who had succeeded in the cleaning, and had brought themselves into a light level contamination.

Those who remain medium level, who did not do the work of cleaning properly, will be destroyed with the heavily contaminated ones.

All that remains now is the group of light contamination level, and if they wish to save themselves, they must go through the Ba'abs, or Star Gates, into other dimensions, so that they could be evaluated by the Anunnaki. If they can be cleaned, they go back to earth. If not, they will live out their lives in another dimension, where conditions are much like our own earth before the cleaning.

They will lead a normal life, but will not be able to reproduce, so eventually they will die out. As for those who go through the Ba'abs, the procedure is extremely difficult. Ba'abs exist everywhere.

There are huge, magnificent Ba'abs that are used regularly by the Anunnaki to cross from one dimension to another. But there are also small ones, located in the street, in a tree, in an apartment building, in your own home, you name it.

They will become visible when the bubble clashes with the earth, and those who were not taken into the bubble,

or were not destroyed, must find their way into a Ba'ab.
All Ba'abs look the same – they are a circle of shifting
light of rainbow colors, very clearly defined. People
wishing to enter a Ba'ab must hurl themselves against it,
and it will open and absorb any number of travelers. As
soon as you enter the Ba'ab, you are already in another
dimension.

It is extremely frightening, a deep blackness illuminated
by explosions, thunderbolts, and streaking comets.

There is a very high level of a stormy, whoosh-like
sound – the noise can be deafening – and the traveler is
swept with violent speed forward, unable to resist or
help the move, and constantly twirled and twisted in one
direction, and then the other.

The traveler will feel dizzy, disoriented, and scared, and
this lasts for an indefinite amount of time. When this
part is over, the traveler is thrown by a huge gust of
wind into a tunnel, which is so brightly lit by orange,
yellow, and white light, it is impossible to keep one's
eyes open for more than a few seconds at a time. The
traveler hears horrible shrieks, screams, and howling of
wind, and when the eyes are open, he or she sees bizarre
faces, weird creatures, and unknown vehicles which
always seem almost on the verge of colliding with the
traveler, but somehow never do.

After a while, the traveler is thrown out of the tunnel
into solid ground, which may be quite painful but not
permanently harmful. The light becomes normal and the
sounds stop.

At that point, the travelers have reached their
destination. It looks much like earth, but it is empty of
people or animals, and plants and houses look very dim,
as if the traveler found himself in virtual reality. Then,
the traveler begins to see people materialize against the
cardboard like background. This takes time, the images

of people float as if from thin air, but then, all of a sudden, reality shifts and the travelers find themselves in a real world.

The animals, incidentally, will never materialize.

All of them have been returned to earth, to their proper places, as mentioned before.

They are not needed here, since no animal labor or the eating of animals is permitted by the Anunnaki, who abhor such practices. In this dimension, the travelers will meet a few Anunnaki, who will direct them to their evaluation and possible cleaning. We do not know how this procedure works, and in truth, it does not matter very much, since only those who made it would be returned to earth.

Those who cannot be cleaned will be sent, through a Ba'ab, to the dimension we have mentioned before, where they will live out their lives, but will not be able to reproduce. The Anunnaki do not wish to kill them, since they are not inherently evil like the heavily contaminated ones.

But they cannot let them reproduce the bad DNA; the Anunnaki do not indulge in sentimental pity, and are fully aware that any form of evil should not be allowed to exist.

***   ***   ***

36-What Is Going To Happen To Organized Religions?

The Answer

- The very first thing the Anunnaki will do when they land on earth will be the reorganization of the human race, readjusting the structure and substructure of our societies.
- The Anunnaki believe that without a new social order, humanity will remain in chaotic state and violent conditions.
- The first change they will bring to earth consist in totally eliminating organized religions, for instance, the Vatican will be reduced to a historic icon. Churches, temples, synagogues, ashrams and particularly beautiful cathedrals will become public libraries and centers for the fine arts.
- The Anunnaki will explain to the human race that the God we worshipped on earth was an invention of the primitive minds of the early human race.
- Anunnaki will explain to the human race that the idea of one god, master of the universe, originated from the belief in many gods in the early days of the history of humanity but for several reasons, the number of deities shrunk to one.

227

- The early prophets, and some of the founders of great religions, saw the Anunnaki as gods. For example, Enki became Yahweh.
- And before Yahweh, he was all sort of things, such as Adon, Adonis, Melkart, Zeus, Brahma, you name it. So the foundation of religion was a fragment of imagination of primitive and uninformed and confused minds of the human race.
- However, something good came out of it, such as the Christian charity, the Jewish Tzedakah, the Buddhist non-violence philosophy, the Islamic protection of the orphans and forgiveness.
- All these virtues, although they are no longer in use today, were a positive aspect of the invention of religion.
- There will be no more churches, synagogues, or any other centers of worship. All that will be replaced by the concept of God as All-That-Is.
- All the famous "Stars" of religion, such as televangelists, fanatic extremists, those who advocate phantasmagorical ideologies such as the Rapture, etc., will have been eliminated.

*** *** ***

37-How Will The Earth Be Protected From Further Contamination From The Grays?

The Answer

- The Anunnaki will create an electro-plasma-laser shield around the orbit of the earth, preventing any hostile extraterrestrial civilization from conquering earth.
- The shield will be an invisible "plasmic belt" surrounding the whole planet earth.
- The "plasmic belt" will look like like a zone of extremely extensive heat that will melt anything that might try to go through it.
- On the inside, the mind of the human beings will be constantly monitored by Anunnaki societies on earth, which report directly to the High Council on Nibiru.
- A new "Conduit" will be implanted in the brain cells of each human, so a new "form" of a "global truth" governing the whole earth, and based totally on scientific facts will shape up social code and ethics, thus eliminating erroneous personal interpretations of law and order. It is no longer special interest groups, influential lobbying organizations, and powerful lawmakers will dictate laws and influence jurisdictions.

231

- The Anunnaki believe that a negative and a malicious mind is as dangerous as an atomic weapon.
- Therefore, he Anunnaki will eliminate all forms of governmental institutions, installations and places, such as NATO, European military posts, strategic ballistic (missiles and nukes) launching pads and bases, The White House, City Halls, European Fund, The Internal Revenue Service, the KGB, the CIA, International Money Fund, the United Nations, World Bank, mansions for governors, so called palaces of justice, and military high command centers, and all establishments that reflect authority over people and create fear in the hearts and minds of populations. They will disappear. And since they will no longer exist, a greater sense of security and feeling of personal autonomy, freedom, and new sense of individual security will come to life.
- The Anunnaki will eliminate all the dangerous secret organizations controlled by entities such as the New World Order, and the Grays who are currently working with official authorities and military scientists in many centers in the U.S., on the surface, underwater, and underground, all potential dangers and risks of war, as well as threat to humanity peace and happiness, such as global military confrontations, invading other countries, tortures, executing officials and heads of states of foreign countries, dominating world markets, greedy monetary systems, atomic annihilation, thus elevating the human race to a higher standard of spirituality, cosmic awareness, and global peace on earth.

- Nations will no longer be judged by their super military power and military might, but by the creative accomplishment of the mind, collective consciousness of their people, and their contribution to the human race as "one race" on earth.
- People will no longer be judged, assessed and rated by the color of their skin, physical looks, wealth, assets, eminence and the importance of positions and status they enjoy and monopolize.

*** *** ***

38-How Will The Human Mind Benefit From The Anunnaki Connection?

The Answer

How Will The Human Mind Benefit From The Anunnaki Connection?

- What the Anunnaki will do will not impose on you new beliefs that bring chaos to your mind, and/or confuse you in your daily transactions.
- The Anunnaki will delete those beliefs that were created by institutions that deprived you physically, mentally, and spiritually from evolving, such as the belief or concept that without confessing your sins to your priest you will not be absolved from your sins and you will not enter the kingdom of God, or such as if you don't convert to Islam, and follow the message of the Prophet Muhammad, you will not enter Heaven.
- Those are the concepts that have controlled the mind of humans for centuries. By demonstrating scientifically and physically what really works, what really is the "honest truth for humanity", the human mind will be given the opportunity to see the whole truth.
- All be based on scientific explanation, and since the mind will evolve, by conquering new scientific frontiers, the spectrum of the human intelligence will increase infinitely.
- Therefore, the human mind will have an extremely developed center of knowledge, and

will tap into the depot of collective intelligence, and consequently voluntarily selects what fits and meets the physical, spiritual, mental and intellectual needs of the person.

*** *** ***

39-Is It A Mind Control Situation?

The Answer

In a previous answer, you say: "A new Conduit will be implanted in the brain cells of each human, so one kind of truth based totally on scientific truth will shape up social code and ethics, thus eliminating erroneous personal interpretation of law and peace."

That sounds like a new form of mind control and like an incredible invasion of each person's privacy. How do you explain that?

- In a way, yes, we will be controlled for a limited amount of time.
- Each individual will have a different time of such control, which will only last until the more advanced faculties will be developed.
- This involves hard work on the part of each human, but the rewards, as mentioned in a previous answer, will be vastly greater than the effort.
- One must remember that having the "Conduit" allows one to connect with the Akashic Records, the greatest depot of knowledge imaginable.
- Some of us will develop faster than others, but since only those who have no Grays' contamination will survive anyway, they will be more than ready to understand the need for such

241

temporary control, that will greatly improve the human race.
- The Anunnaki themselves have a telepathic connection to each other, the same as will be imposed on us, and they know how to use it with discretion and ethical behaviour.

*** *** ***

40-How Will The "Conduit" Be Installed? Does it require surgical operation?

Is this a kind of implanting a third eye in our brain as some Hindu and Buddhist talked about?

The Answer

How The "Conduit" will be installed? Does it require surgical operation? Is this a kind of implanting a third eye in our brain as some Hindu and Buddhist talked about?

- Installing the "Conduit" in the brain cells does not require a surgical operation.
- In terrestrial terms, it's like activating your cellular phone without going to the telephone company.
- It's like transferring money from your account to another account, without going physically to a bank, carrying money bills and notes, and physically giving this amount to a bank clerk to deposit it in another account.
- It is transferred automatically via wire, a non physical operation.
- But with the Anunnaki, it will be a higher level of a more advanced technology, that the human mind will understand in due time.

*** *** ***

41-What Will Happen To The Teachings Of Jesus, Moses, Mohammed, And Buddha, If The Anunnaki Demolish All Religions And Our Religious Beliefs Systems?

The Answer

What Will Happen To The Teachings Of Jesus, Moses, Mohammed, And Buddha, If The Anunnaki Demolish All Religions And Our Religious Beliefs Systems?

- The Anunnaki will abolish all forms of organized religions, but not the code of ethics, fairness, and justice.
- For instance, the mind will be fertilized with a device that will enable the human being to tap into a higher sphere of knowledge.
- One example would be the possibility of mankind to go back in time and listen exactly to what the founders of religion have said. Not what their followers have created as doctrines and dogma for their own benefits and personal interests.
- Religious systems based upon organized establishments will be eliminated.
- The human mind will be able through the implanted "Conduit" and the "Miraya" to go back to the time of Jesus and listen to his sermons and teachings. Humans will go back in time, and will see Jesus walking in the streets of Nazareth, Bethlehem, and Jerusalem, and they will be able to listen to him at Mount Olive, and by doing so, they will be able to retrieve the true message. They will compare the teachings of

249

Jesus, automatically, with what the Church, its doctors, its bishops, and its governments, invented and fabricated. They will have the two versions, the original one, and the new one invented by organized religions.

- In summary, the Anunnaki are not abolishing religions because they will be taking us straight to the original message of religions, to the very source.
- Instead, they will eliminate the bureaucratic, governmental, financial, and business aspect created by those who became the custodians of religions, and unfortunately, erroneously, influenced our mind, ethics and way of life.

*** *** ***

42-You Said That The Anunnaki Will Impose On Humans a Vegetarian Diet. So what will replace meat?

Will the Anunnaki give us new directions about feeding the world with soy, wheat, etc.?

The Answer

You Said That The Anunnaki Will Impose On Humans a Vegetarian Diet. So what will replace meat? Will the Anunnaki give us new directions about feeding the world with soy, wheat, etc.?...

- Although many anthropologists, scientists and doctors of nutrition made it clear that the human body needs meat for physical and mental development, because they found out that back in history when our early ancestors started to eat meat, their brain size increased, and their mental faculties developed rapidly, and while this is true, humans who kill animals and eat their flesh will be forever isolated from cosmic civilizations which are more developed, richer, and more rewarding.
- In the eyes of the Anunnaki, only savage creatures kill other living creatures (Referring to animals) to feed themselves.
- Anunnaki do not advocate eating meat, because it deprives living creatures from living. And by their standard it is a crime.
- However, taking into consideration the physical development needs of the human body, the Anunnaki will substitute meat with a new sort of sea food that will grow in the sea and which will

253

have the taste of fish, and also all the necessary nutrients.

- Also, they will develop certain DNA in trees, capable of producing milk-like substance and fruit that will taste exactly like meat, and it would be much more nutritious, and beneficial to the physical and mental needs of humans.

*** *** ***

43-What Will Happen To The Vast Numbers Of Animals That Used To Live In Farms For Consumption Purposes, And Are No Longer Consumed, Since Everyone Is Vegetarian?

The Answer

What Will Happen To The Vast Numbers Of Animals That Used To Live In Farms For Consumption Purposes, And Are No Longer Consumed, Since Everyone Is Vegetarian?

- They will have a very peaceful life, like many of the animals that currently live on Nibiru such as cats, butterflies, and a wide variety of birds and aquatic creatures in the seas.
- Anunnaki, when they created humans, they installed minds instead of feelings.
- The Anunnaki did not find animals to be communicative and intelligent in general, and they based their judgement on those monstrous beasts that roamed the earth at its dawn, such as dinosaurs and crocodiles, which incidentally, were not created by the Anunnaki. So when many of us will no longer exist on earth, nor in other dimensions, the animals will be left in peace to live out their lives, but will not reproduce any further.
- Animals will become self-sufficient because the Anunnaki will allow them to regain part of their lost animal kingdom.

*** *** ***

44-What Will Happen To All The Homeless Pets, Whose Infected Owners Were Destroyed?

The Answer

What Will Happen To All The Homeless Pets, Whose Infected Owners Were Destroyed?

- The animals have a sort of animal conduit that intuitively will link them to animal communities.
- They will join the newly established animal kingdoms in areas where humans will not have access to.
- The animals will be relocated to places in zones where they will not be exposed to dangers from other, bigger animals that could devour them.
- Because the Anunnaki consciously will alter the DNA of humans to a degree where the human race will lose taste and interest in meat, the same thing will happen with animals, big and small.
- It will be an earthy-cosmic cleansing in taste and physical priorities.
- The animal will live on natural resources on earth.

***   ***   ***

45-What Will Happen On Earth During The Final Clash With The Anunnaki?

The Answer

What Will Happen On Earth During The Final Clash With The Anunnaki?

- As we have explained in a previous answer, the Anunnaki will start the cataclysmic event of 2022 by removing all the clean, uncontaminated humans, all the animals, the plants, and the inanimate objects they wish to preserve, by taking them into the bubble they have brought to clash with the earth.

- This bubble is made of non-destructive, anti-matter like substance, and it will protect everything placed in it from harm, until the cleansing of the earth will be completed. We have also explained what would happen to those humans who are only lightly contaminated.

- They will go through the Ba'abs, or Stargates, to face a journey into the unknown, with the hope of being cleaned and saved. They have no guarantee, but going through the Ba'abs and risking their lives is the only chance they have.

- The question remaining now is, what is going to happen to those who have remained on earth – those who are contaminated with evil to the extent that they cannot be saved?

- First, one must remember that in an instant, the houses these people lived in, any animal that they have had, all the plants of the earth, and

264

many other buildings, will disappear in a blink of an eye.

- For a short time, these people will find themselves in an environment that is already totally alien and frightening.
- Some may remember the warnings of the Anunnaki, started fourteen years before the event and constantly repeated but ignored by many. Others may have never even noticed the warnings, and so they have no clue as to what is happening.
- None of that matters, since one must also remember that these people are evil to the core, that nothing can reclaim them because they have nothing which is good in their minds, and that the Anunnaki have absolutely no mercy and no sentimentality about evil and its redemption.
- The Anunnaki firmly believe that all evil should be destroyed, if at all possible.
- At this point, the sun and the moon, depending on the time zones, would seem to be eclipsed.
- This will not happen naturally, but rather, the whole sky, over the entire world, will be covered with spaceships and mother spaceships.
- A massive ceiling of metal shapes of machinery, gadgets, wheels, and shifting lights will be created.
- They will be ominously silent, as if waiting. Looking at this from below will be so frightening that many people will lose their heads.
- Some will try to hide, some will run around in circles, not knowing where to go. In crowded, urban areas, they will create stampedes, killing each other in the process.

- Others will run into their churches, trying to pray, and the churches will ring their bells.
- Some of the religious leaders were saved or gone through the Ba'abs, and so have disappeared already.
- Those who are false and contaminated will still try to call their congregations, feeling that perhaps that would be a way to salvation.
- In various cities, people will try to reach their governments, without much success.
- The only officials that have stayed on their posts will issue orders to avoid any interference with the extraterrestrials, since it will make everything even more dangerous and no one on earth has the technology to match.
- The officials' orders will be ignored, particularly by those in rural areas, who are used to self sufficiency.
- These people will confront the Anunnaki, start shooting at them with their guns.
- As in other areas, which of course have had many good people living in them, only the violent ones have remained, since the others have already escaped.
- Acting stupidly, they will annoy the Anunnaki with their inept shooting until the Anunnaki decide to paralyze them with special beams of light, for a limited time.
- When the beams' effects wear off, some will resume their doomed attempts to fight, and at this point the Anunnaki will go into the final stage.
- From the bottom of the spaceships, they will diffuse a special substance that will land in huge, swirling streams.

- It is a black liquid, mixed with light and electricity, and some strange sparkling particles, which are a form of energy or radiation.
- It smells like fire and brimstone, but strangely, it is cold to the touch. Yet, it burns everything that touches it.
- This is a tool of annihilation, a tool that no one can fight.
- The substance will slither inexorably over the ground, the buildings, and the stranded cars like icy cold lava waves.
- It will sweep away many people, killing them instantly. Once it covers a large area, it will begin to coagulate, and as it does so, will expand and rise up, foot by foot, until it reaches the height of eight storied buildings.
- Slowly, it will harden, solidifying itself into steel-like state.
- Huge stacks of smoke will rise up into the sky, cars will melt, buildings will collapse, and fires will start everywhere, not only by the touch of the substance, but spontaneously, when the wind carries the particles of energy into flammable materials.
- The fire and brimstone smell will now mix with that of burning flesh and of melting metal, plastic and rubber.
- Then, all of a sudden, the substance will stop growing, and assume the appearance of craggy mountains, with sharp edges and canyons.
- The very few who have escaped, who have now nowhere to go to, will try to climb on the substance, since the earth itself will be buried in it.

- This will be futile, since the substance will be too slippery for the climb.
- They will start to fall and slip, and be instantly killed.
- These conditions will continue all over the entire world for two days; no one will be left alive on the scorched earth.
- On the third day, all the spaceships will leave, and in twenty-four hours, the substance and all it consumed will turn to dust.
- The earth will be ready for the vast cleaning. For that purpose, other spaceships will appear, of completely different appearance.
- The new ones will not be circular like the others, but crescent shaped, and of pleasant colors, nothing frightening about them.
- They will activate the vacuum system that we have mentioned in a previous answer, to ready the earth for a new life.

*** *** ***

46-Are The Anunnaki Going To Change Our Way Of Life?

Are the Anunnaki going to change the way we do business, what we do to make a living, and are they going to create or abolish some professional institutions?

The Answer

Are The Anunnaki Going To Change Our Way Of Life?
Are the Anunnaki going to change the way we do business, what we do to make a living, and are they going to create or abolish some professional institutions?

- This will be one of the most significant changes that humanity will see, because the Anunnaki will not support any of our greed-infested systems.
- The most profound change will be the abolition of money and every system that is attached to money.
- People will work in their chosen professions (or a new profession that they will adopt, more on that later in this answer) and produce or serve as usual.
- They will not be paid, but they will have everything that they need. Everyone will have a comfortable home, designed to his or her taste.
- Good food for us and for our pets, beautiful clothes, nice jewelry, cosmetics, diapers for the babies, toys, hobby supplies, etc. will always be available in huge cooperatives that will look like

excellent supermarkets, open day and night so that no one will ever lack.

- What we consider luxury items will also be available – the Anunnaki have no desire to have us live in austerity.
- We can always have books, TV, radio, home films, etc. We can go to the theater, the ballet, the symphony orchestra, chamber music performances, movies – always for free.
- The only thing the Anunnaki will deprives us off is *excess*.
- There will be no need for hoarding, since everything will always be available, but you will not be able to be richer than your neighbor. Equality will be established, and appreciated by those of us who are not contaminated by the greed and meanness of the Grays.
- Since money will no longer signify, obviously there will not be a need to have places like Fort Knox.
- It is going to be destroyed, and the gold used for ornamental purposes. That is the only reason people will value gold now – its beauty.
- A good artist can create some pretty good pieces from such lovely substance, which will be so widely available after the great change. The same will happen, incidentally, with diamonds, and other gems. Their intrinsic value will disappear, so jewelry will only be appreciated for its intricate and elegant design, not for how many carats a stone weighs.
- Because of that, there will be no need for the IRS, the Social Security system, and other such organizations. The elimination of the money

system will cause many professions to disappear, such as:

- Accountants
- Bankers
- Tax preparers
- Security guards
- IRS employees

But money will not be the only "victim." In a society that consists of good people, people who have no need or desire to commit any crime whatsoever, there will be no need for the legal system.

All organizations pertaining to the law will disappear, including the Supreme Court.

And of course, no prisons. This will eliminate many professions:

- Lawyers
- Judges
- Court clerks
- Prison officials and guards

All governments will be abolished. No elected officials, no presidents, no kings. People who are good do not need anyone telling them how to live, they do it instinctively. This will eliminate thousands of positions:

- Presidents

- Kings
- Governors
- Mayors
- All government employees
- Social workers
- Child agencies

Since the Anunnaki technology is going to keep us healthy, there will be no need for hospitals or clinics, other than those devoted to childbirth, and much of the work there will be done without the need for people. In addition, there will not be any incidents of mental health. This will eliminate the positions of most doctors and nurses, and of additional employees such as:

- Hospital administration
- Hospital billing
- Psychiatrists
- Psychologists
- Hospital janitors

For transportation, we will no longer have the need for cars and airplanes. There will be advanced technology that will allow us a much more efficient forms of transportation and the use of clean and efficient energy, but in the process, we will eliminate the need for any fossil fuels. This will eliminate many professions, such as:

- Gas stations
- Agencies supplying us with electricity and gas
- Car manufacturers
- Airplane manufacturers
- Highway builders

In addition, there will be some miscellaneous professions that will not remain, since they will no longer be appreciated or needed.

For example, the fashion industry, with its cruel attempts to make women into slaves of someone else's ideas of beauty, will entirely disappear. Beautiful clothing will be created by individual designers or by any one who likes to indulge in it as a creative hobby.

Advertising, of course, will vanish as well. These miscellaneous jobs that will be eliminated include:

- Runway models
- Beauty contest organizers
- Manicurists
- Cosmetologists
- Advertising commercials actors and voice over artists

This situation should not cause alarm. Those who will lose their professions will be trained for another profession, always entirely of their choice, that will give them pleasure and pride to pursue. Even those who have not lost their profession, but who feel the need for a change, will be encouraged to pursue a career change. As a matter of fact, since the life expectancy of each and every person will be greatly increased, it is expected that many people will have numerous career changes as time goes by. Life long study is always encouraged by the Anunnaki, who consider the acquisition of knowledge the most enjoyable thing a person can do.

Many professions will change in the way they are perceived. For example, the teaching profession, for both children and adults, will become the most highly respected profession in the world.
Librarians will be very highly regarded.
Gardeners will be of great importance.
Historians and writers will be greatly valued. But of course, in a world that judges a person by what he or she is, not by how much money is accumulated, every profession will be appreciated for its usefulness to the entire community.

*** *** ***

47-How Do Anunnaki Explain The Relationship Between Jesus and Mary Magdalene?

The Answer

The Holy Grail topic occupies a paramount part in the Anunnaki manuscript "The Book of Rama-Dosh", because many early Christian thinkers and Gnostics were members of Ulema groups and their affiliates, such as the Cathars, the Templars, and the Knights of St. John Order of Malta.

Logically, the followers of Mary Magdalene who created the first "Christian group" in Alexandria, and later on joined the Ulema became interested in the Anunnaki.

Because the Anunnaki society is matriarchal in essence, Mary Magdalene figures prominently in its literature.

For centuries, in the Near East, Middle East, North Africa, Asia Minor, Anatolia and the early Coptic, Aramaic, Syriac, Nabatean, and Anunnaki circles and learned societies, the New Testament was followed, and understood quite differently from the way contemporary Western believers, devoted Christians and hard-core doctors of the Roman Catholic Church do.

In addition to the Gospel of Mary which contained only a few pages about her life, her ministry and relationship

279

with Jesus, several other manuscripts told the true story of Jesus, Mary Magdalene and Christianity. Many of those early religious manuscripts were written by Ulema.

The Ulema circle which consisted of some of the brightest minds of the era who came from various and different cultural, social and religious backgrounds, told the absolute truth about Jesus and Mary Magdalene. Many Ulema were Muslims, Christians, Hindu, Buddhists, Gnostics and free-spirited thinkers and ethicists.

However, they shared many things in common, such as the truthful knowledge and essence of the religions that were originated in the Levant (Orient, Middle and Near East), the origin of mankind, the nature of the Anunnaki, substances that compose parallel dimensions, and the concept of "human salvation."

Their knowledge extended to the Old Testament, the New Testament, extraterrestrial civilizations, and the destined future of mankind.

To the Roman Catholic Church, the knowledge and teachings of these enlightened teachers were sacrilege and blasphemy...in other words, a direct and an imminent threat to Rome.

The Ulema who taught the principles and code of ethic as prescribed in the Anunnaki Rama-Dosh" book had an ultimate respect for Jesus and Mary Magdalene. However, the Ulema never considered Jesus of Nazareth as a Messiah or God.

In "Revelation of an Anunnaki's Wife", a biography of Victoria, a hybrid woman, half human and half Anunnaki, I co-authored with Ilil Arbel, Ph.D., we devoted an extensive chapter on the relationship between Jesus and Mary Magdalene. What we wrote about was based upon revelations by Victoria depicting her travel in time, to Marseille, where allegedly she met

Mary Magdalene in her own home. Please refer to the book. But briefly, the Ulema/Anunnaki were fully aware of the relationship that existed between Jesus and Mary Magdalene as a married couple.

This leads me to several questions and inquiries I have received from my readers who asked whether Jesus was God, the Son of God, or an Anunnaki?

The Rama-Dosh book describes Jesus as a Rabbi who preached love, compassion and justice.

But also, the Rama-Dosh book depicted Jesus as a rebel with a revolutionary set of mind, however peaceful and loving...

No, Jesus was not an Anunnaki. And Jesus was not God. The cliché "Son of God" was frequently used by the Essenes in their teachings, and was used to refer to the "righteous ones."

The teachings of the Anunnaki-Ulema did not diminish the importance of Christianity, nor tarnish the image of Jesus. Simply, they shed the light of truth on the origin of Christianity, the nature of Jesus and the important role, Mary Magdalene played in launching this great religion in Alexandria, and her paramount impact on Jesus.

The Roman Catholic Church felt threatened, and feared that its authority over the simple minded and illiterate believers will dissipate.

Christianity as we know it today in the West, is a scenario well-crafted by Emperor Constantine and the mighty Vatican. It is absolutely misinterpreted, fabricated and intentionally re-created by the Roman Catholic Church.

Christianity was never created by Jesus. Christianity is the product and the results of the propaganda of Paul.

281

The Anunnaki Book of Rama-Dosh, as well as the Anunnaki Miraya (Sort of Akashic Records, so to speak) tell the true story of Jesus, his life in Palestine, Arwad, Phoenicia, Cyprus and France. Also, it describes in detail the episodes of the life Mary Magdalene and Jesus shared in Palestine and France.

Mary Magdalene, The Wife of Jesus:

"The Book of Rama-Dosh" describes Mary Magdalene as a relatively young, attractive, and faithful Jewish woman who stood by her man (Jesus).
She was the wife of Jesus and their matrimonial union gave birth to healthy children who grew up in Marseille, France. Long time before any book was written in the West about the Holy Grail and Jesus bloodlines, the remnants and descendants of the Anunnaki in the Middle and Near East already told us that Jesus was married, Mary Magdalene was his wife, and the concept of the Holy Grail was nothing else but the lineage of Jesus. These facts were well known and accepted during the first 3 centuries A.D. in the eastern countries.

The Anunnaki literature is not limited exclusively to space-time travel, the genetic creation of the human race, and the captivating Sumerian mythology.
It has also, deep emotions, a human touch, and captivating philosophical, religious, and metaphysical aspects.
After all, many of the ethical codes and laws of societies of the ancient world were given by the Anunnaki to rulers and kings in the Near East, Middle East, Asia and North Africa, including Mesopotamia's King Hammurabi, India's king Dabshalim, Persia's shah Anu Sherwan Kesra, Tyre's King, Hiram, and King Solomon.

However, the Anunnaki did not give the human races laws governing religions and faith, even though some of the lower class of the early Anunnaki who descended on earth brought to the humanity organized religions and fake deities. They had to do it in order to control and enslave humanity.

The purpose of bringing those religions to earth was to create fear in the minds and hearts of primitive humans.

The early Anunnaki knew that religion is the most effective way and method to control people. And when you religiously control people, you get hold of their lives, way of life, assets, and possessions, present and future. The Roman Catholic Church knew that quite well and practiced these tactics for centuries.

Consequently, any book, any manuscript, any text, any teaching that taught the truth, the factual origin of man, the creation, science, astronomy, studies of the future of humanity, became a direct threat to the power and authority of Rome and its affiliates around the world.

Books by Maximillien de Lafayette
Published by Times Square Press. Elite Associates International

---

Description and Explanation of Anunnaki, Babylonian, Sumerian, Akkadian, Assyrian, Phoenician Slabs, Seals, Inscriptions, Statues, Tablets and Secret Symbols

The first book ever written about Babylon, Sumer, Phoenicia, Hittites and the Anunnaki slabs, tablets/inscriptions. Based on the original work, writings and lectures of Ulema de Lafayette from 1962 to the present. Each artifact is described, translated and explained. A major masterpiece!

The world's first documentation on the existence of the extraterrestrial gods who created our civilizations. Hundreds of photos & illustrations. This book was written to deal with and to explain all the meanings, mysteries and secrets of ancient civilizations connected with the Anunnaki, and to provide the readers with sufficient guidance, translation and explanation of major archeological finds, ranging from a figurine to a massive monument.

*** *** ***

The Complete, Revised and Expanded Ulema Anunnaki Tarot. Extraterrestrial Lessons and Techniques to See your Future

For the first time ever in the Western world, and in the history of the occult, divination, Tarot, Anunnaki, Ulema, and esoteric studies of all kinds, the reader, the seer, the adept and the novice will have access to the world's most powerful book on the subject. These

7,000 year old secrets, and forbidden knowledge and techniques, for reading the future and changing major events in your life, are being made available for the first time.

Lessons, advice, techniques, training and reading your Future and Tarot are directly provided by the last contemporary Ulema Anunnaki who lived consecutively through three centuries.

Techniques and lessons include how to discover your lucky hours and days; how to reverse bad luck; learning about your past lives, your present, your future, and your multiple existences on Earth and in other dimensions, how to foresee and avert imminent dangers threatening your life, health, career, business, and relationships.

***   ***   ***

The Revised, Indexed and Complete Book of the Anunnaki-Ulema Final Warning to Humanity, the End of Time, and the Return of the Anunnaki in 2022.

The Grays' creation of a hybrid-human race, and the final clash between extraterrestrials and Earth.

Detailed descriptions of:

1-When and how the Anunnaki will return to Earth;

2-Areas/countries of their landing;

3-What their agenda is;

4-What they are going to do to the human race;

5-Who is going to be saved and/or killed;

6-Their spaceships and stargates (Ba'abs) over major cities;

7-The 2022 major arrival of the Anunnaki to Earth and their clash with humans;

8-Holographic pictures showing the entire sequence of the Roswell crash;

9-Inside the Dulce Base;

10-The Anunnaki's classification of Humanity into three groups, regarding their level of contamination;
11-United States "Protocol on the Extraterrestrial visit to Earth in 2022";
12-United States Government publications on extraterrestrial invasions.

*** *** ***

Mind-Bending Black Operations, Weapons Systems and Experiments by Extraterrestrials, Grays and Governments: The Hidden World of the Anunnaki, Ulema, Grays and Secret Military-Aliens Bases and Laboratories on Earth, Underwater and in Space

An explosive book on secret projects and black operations conducted by extraterrestrials and the Gray alien race living here on planet Earth. Detailed listing of each project, and explanation of its impact on the human race.
It includes:
1-B.C.B: The horrible "Compressor" and the alien-US technology: Sucking up your brain, memory and all your personal thoughts.
2-Weapons systems capable of slowing down time, or prolonging it indefinitely.
3-Bioelectric extraterrestrial robots "B.E.R": The Humanoids-US "BER Program" and Men-in-Black.
4-Extraterrestrials' "Corridor Plasma".
5-The Vortex Tunnel: The American military has successfully sent six men through the vortex. 6-Extraterrestrial genetic labs that created half humans/half animals.

*** *** ***

The New and Revised Book on Ulema Secret Teachings on Anunnaki, Extraterrestrials, UFOs,

Alien Civilizations and how to Acquire Paranormal Powers

For the first time, Maximillien de Lafayette reveals and explains the secrets of the Anunnaki who created the human race some 65,000 years ago. A rare opportunity to enter their secret world hidden from us for the past 7,000 years. It analyses and explains step by step, the brightest and darkest secrets and mysteries of the origin of the human race, who created us, and how the Holly Scriptures borrowed their stories from the Anunnaki-Ulema books.

*** *** ***

Anunnaki, UFOs, Extraterrestrials And Afterlife Greatest Information As Revealed By Maximillien de Lafayette. A set of 3 books

Book 1: Anunnaki, UFOs, Extraterrestrials And Afterlife Greatest Information As Revealed By Maximillien de Lafayette. Part 1.

Summary of the best of Maximillien de Lafayette, the world's leading authority on the Anunnaki, and selections of his most important writings, mind-blowing discoveries and findings about:

1-Anunnaki greatest secrets,
2-Extraterrestrials habitat and way of life on their planets,
3-UFOs and USOs technology,
4-Year 2022 date of the Anunnaki return to earth,
5-US President meeting with aliens,
6-Allegedly a fake God we worship (Judaic-Christian-Muslim God),
7-How aliens created us genetically from clay,
8-Description of the afterlife,
9-How to contact dead loved ones and pets,

10-humans and aliens living in parallel worlds,

11-Galactic copies of ourselves in multiple universes,

12-Anunnaki Ulema secret techniques of longevity, health and immortality,

13-How Moses and Abraham selected and created a God from the Sumerian/Phoenician pantheon, and much much more.

This massive work in 4 parts is a presentation of the best ideas, research and discoveries taken from 60 previously written books by the legendary Maximillien de Lafayette.

Book 2: Anunnaki, UFOs, Extraterrestrials And Afterlife Greatest Information As Revealed By Maximillien de Lafayette. Part 2. 4th Edition

It includes:

1. Anunnaki's karma.

2. Entering The 4th Dimension And Returning From The World Beyond.

3. How do Anunnaki measure time?

4. The Anunnaki have created us on earth to serve their needs.

5. Earth is considered the lowest organic and human life-form in the universe.

6. If your name contains one of the 72 powerful words of the Al Khalek (Creator), then you will be lucky, and you will prosper in life.

7. The origin and the genetic creation of the human races by the Anunnaki.

8. The space-made human creatures.

9. Anunnaki used an extraction from mushroom and mixed it with an Anunnaki female's DNA to create a secret race of creature.

10. Female extraterrestrial goddesses created us, not Jehovah, God or Allah.

Book 3: Anunnaki, UFOs, Extraterrestrials And Afterlife Greatest Information As Revealed By Maximillien de Lafayette. Part 3. 4th Edition
It contains:
1. The genetic composition of Abel.
2. Eve's relation to the Anunnaki.
3. The afrit, Djins and evil spirits.
4. Arakh-nara "Arcturus" and Edgar Cayce.
5. A selection of important words from the Anunnaki's language.
6. Building the Anunnaki's tool "Minzar" to see the future and enter another dimension.
7. Contacting the alternate realities.
8. Secret calendar of the Anunnaki.
9. How real is the holographic/parallel dimension you are visiting, after using the Anunnaki time-space tool?
10. The Anunnaki Miraya and opening the Conduit.

*** *** ***

Mind Blowing Dialogues With Anunnaki Ulema Masters Living Among Us. 3rd Edition. Revelations of the Greatest Information, Secrets & Mysteries of UFOs, Extraterrestrials, Time Space Travel, Parallel Dimensions, Occult and Life After Death
3rd Edition, brand new and revised.
For the first time in the history of modern ufology and Anunnaki, real people communicate with 300/500 year old Anunnaki-Ulema and write to them, read their correspondence, questions& answers.
Are you protected by an angel, a "Double", your astral body? The whole secrets and story of the German first UFOs, frontiers of the world beyond; Nibiru, the Anunnaki's physical and non-Physical dimensions.
Matrix of humanity, Matrix of the Universe, Matrix of your life & future. Description of how Anunnaki created

Mankind. This is what you see & feel when you enter Nibiru, the afterlife & other dimensions.

Description of Grays fetuses storage room, tubes & containers, operation room for breeding, hybridization, creating new race. Complete description of the habitat of hybrids, cloned people, how they live day by day. Relation between you, Anunnaki and God (is he real or fake?) Why aliens & humans have MIND not a soul?

*** *** ***

THE BOOK OF RAMADOSH.7,000 Year Old Anunnaki Ulema Techniques To Live Longer, Happier, Healthier, Wealthier.

4th and latest edition. Possibly, this is the greatest book on the Anunnaki-Ulema extraordinary powers ever published in the West.

Learn their techniques that will change your life for ever. You will never be the same person again.

This book reveals knowledge that is thousands of years old.

Generally, such a statement would bring to mind images of the occult, hidden mysteries, perhaps ancient religious manuscripts. But the Book of Ramadosh is different.

It is based on "Transmission of Mind", used eons ago by the Anunnaki and their remnants on Earth. Written by Maximillien de Lafayette, author of 250 books, and the world leading authority on Anunnaki/Ulema.

The book not only gives you techniques that could bring you health, happiness, and prosperity, but goes deeply into the why and how these techniques do so. Learn how to revisit past/future & travel in time/space; see dead friends & pets in afterlife; secret hour to open Conduit & zoom into your Double & multiple universes; bring luck and change your future...

*** *** ***

Hollywood's Most Horrible People, Stars, Times, and Scandals. 3rd Edition.
360 photos, huge pics, full page-spread).
Sex scandals that shook Hollywood, USA, Europe and world politics. Names and photos of Hollywood stars and women who slept with John F. Kennedy. Hollywood stars rape and affairs. Scandalous love life of hundreds of stars/celebrities. Hollywood phony and fake "Latin Lovers".
Name of today bisexual/lesbian actresses.
Names of Hollywood sex pests, sex-offenders, actors/actresses of the "Casting Couch" and names of major male actors who seduced male superstars like John Wayne, Clark Gable, Randolph Scott, Montgomery Clift.
Scums and shady characters of American cinema and horrible moguls and studios' executives (Their names & photos).
Everything about members of the "Sewing Circle", the secret group of all the lesbian and bisexual actresses and their group sex, their names and photos. Hollywood worst marriages, name and photos.
Arrests of modern day actors/actresses, conviction/sentences. Stars/celebrities love triangle, names and photos; the cheaters and cheated.

*** *** ***

Hollywood's Earth Shattering Scandals: The infamous, villains, nymphomaniacs and shady character in motion pictures. A set of 2 Volumes.

Volume 1: Hollywood Earth Shattering Scandals. The Infamous, Villains, Nymphomaniacs and Shady Characters in Motion Pictures. Part 1. 4th Edition.

Part 1 of 2 parts.

Largest/biggest book on the market.

There is no other book like it! Comprehensive, illustrated, documented, explosive! Movie stars-heroes and role models who in real life are the scum of the earth. Their names (Males and Females, past and present) nymphomaniacs, homosexuals, lesbians, junkies, drugs addicts, rapists, suicidal, felons and murderers. Their double lives, shady deals, arrests, convictions and mug shots (Larry King, Al Pacino, Bill Gates, Suzanne Somers, Steve McQueen. F. Sinatra, etc.) Name of the women and stars Kennedy slept with. Hollywood repulsive moguls, producers, directors. Greatest scandals in Hollywood's history, past and present. Stars naked ambition. Stars insanity, wild sex parties, orgies, & obsession with money, greed, fame and power, and who are they?

How they did it, when, how, and with whom?

Their names, enter their donjons, and learn everything about their most repulsive life style and way of life.

Volume 2: Hollywood's Earth Shattering Scandals: The infamous, villains, nymphomaniacs and shady character in motion pictures. Part 2. Book 2.

Or in one mega volume (2 Volumes in one)

Mega Volume:
Hollywood Earth Shattering Scandals. The Infamous, Villains, Nymphomaniacs and Shady Characters in Motion Pictures. 3rd Edition.

Books written by Maximillien de Lafayette, available on kindle/wireless

Description, Translation, and Explanation of Babylonian, Sumerian, Akkadian, Assyrian, Ugaritic, Anunnaki and Phoenician Cylinder Seals, Slabs, Inscriptions, Statues, Tablets and Symbols. Part One. 5th Edition.

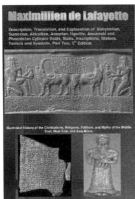

Description, Translation, and Explanation of Babylonian, Sumerian, Akkadian, Assyrian, Ugaritic, Anunnaki and Phoenician Cylinder Seals, Slabs, Inscriptions, Statues, Tablets and Symbols. Part Two. 5th Edition.

The Anunnaki Final Warning to Humanity, the End of Time, and the Return of the Anunnaki in 2022. 6th Edition. The Grays' creation of a hybrid-human race, and the final clash between extraterrestrials and Earth.

The Complete, Revised and Expanded Ulema Anunnaki Tarot. Extraterrestrial Lessons and Techniques to See your Future. 6th Edition: The world's most powerful book on the occult and foreseeing your future on Earth and in other dimensions.

Hollywood's Earth Shattering Scandals: The infamous, villains, nymphomaniacs and shady character in motion pictures. 6th Edition.

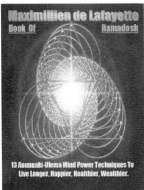

THE BOOK OF RAMADOSH: 13 Anunnaki Ulema Techniques To Live Longer, Happier, Healthier, Wealthier. 7th Edition. Paranormal, alien life, occult, extraterrestrials, UFO, supernatural, ESP, parallel universes. Commentaries and Studies.

Mind Blowing Dialogues With Anunnaki Ulema Masters Living Among Us. 5th Edition. Revelations of the Greatest Information, Secrets & Mysteries of UFOs, Extraterrestrials, Time Space Travel, Parallel Dimensions, Occult and Life After Death.

Anunnaki, UFOs, Extraterrestrials And Afterlife Greatest Information As Revealed By Maximillien de Lafayette. Part 1. 5th Edition. Selections from his 50 years of studying with Anunnaki

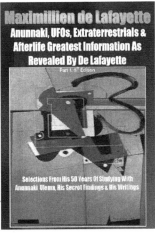

Ulema, his secret findings & his writings.

Anunnaki, UFOs, Extraterrestrials And Afterlife Greatest Information As Revealed By Maximillien de Lafayette. Part 2. 5th Edition. Selections from his 50 years of studying with Anunnaki Ulema, his secret findings & his writings.

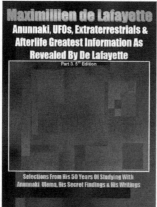
Anunnaki, UFOs, Extraterrestrials And Afterlife Greatest Information As Revealed By Maximillien de Lafayette. Part 3. 5th Edition. Selections from his 50 years of studying with Anunnaki Ulema, his secret findings & his writings.

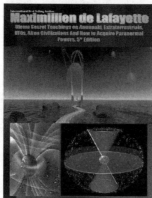
Ulema Secret Teachings on Anunnaki, Extraterrestrials, UFOs, Alien Civilizations and How to Acquire Paranormal Powers. 5th Edition. Supersymetric Mind, Shape-

shifting, Fourth Dimension, Hybrids, Reading the Future.

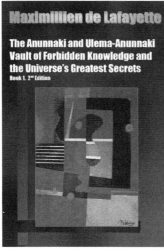

The Anunnaki and Ulema-Anunnaki Vault of Forbidden Knowledge and the Universe's Greatest Secrets. Book 1. 2nd Edition.

The Anunnaki and Ulema-Anunnaki Vault of Forbidden Knowledge and the Universe's Greatest Secrets. Book 2. 2nd Edition.

The Anunnaki and Ulema-Anunnaki Vault of Forbidden Knowledge and the Universe's Greatest Secrets. Book 3. 2nd Edition.

Mind-Bending Black Operations, Weapons Systems and Experiments by Extraterrestrials, Grays and Government. 6th Edition

23054888R00190

Made in the USA
Middletown, DE
16 August 2015